A
TON
OF
MALICE

A
TON
OF
MALICE

THE HALF-LIFE OF
AN IRISH PUNK IN LONDON

BARRY MCKINLEY

First published in Great Britain in 2017 by Old Street Publishing Ltd
Yowlestone House, Tiverton, Devon EX16 8LN
www.oldstreetpublishing.co.uk

ISBN 978-1-910400-53-1

10 9 8 7 6 5 4 3 2 1

A CIP catalogue record for this title is available from the British Library.

Printed and bound in the Czech Republic.

For Mags, John and James

CONT

ENTS

A
TON
OF
MALICE

I

HOME

You should never get stoned when you have to carry a coffin.

My brother Niall squeezed my arm as we left the chapel, and for that I could have slapped the bastard. I shouldered the front left side of the coffin and wobbled under a weight that seemed too great for a woman who by the end had shrunk to the size of a doll. Niall was on the other side, his arm draped weakly around me. I couldn't see his face, and I didn't want to because grief makes people uglier than usual. We walked to the open grave, guided by a man in a black Abercrombie who huffed steam into the cold air.

"Have you been drinking?" hissed Niall, showing how little he knew me. I hadn't been drinking, but earlier that morning I had gone through the medicine cabinet looking for Percocet or Demerol. She must have used it all up in her final agony. Instead I'd smoked a joint under the apple tree in the garden.

"What are you at?" said Niall.

"What do you mean?"

"You're going to the left."

"Am I?"

Niall tugged at the coffin to steer us back on course and I almost dropped it. There was a gasp from the crowd, but I barely heard it. I was miles away, thinking about Kim Sutton in London, imagining her running her fingers through Roland's matted hair. Roland was a yoga instructor.

We stopped at the graveside, where a lone piper was playing a screeching lament.

"Who is that?" I asked.

"That's Cousin Phil," said Niall, his voice made distant by the hard oak and the dead woman between us.

"He looks a right cunt," I said.

"Shut it!"

I hadn't seen Phil since I was a kid and now here he was with a big hairy hat and a cow's stomach under his arm. *Screeee-scraw-scrawdiddly* went the bagpipes. It was a terrible racket, but unfortunately not enough to wake the dead. The coffin sliced through my collarbone and I had a stoned image of Roland sitting in the lotus position in his Kennington flat, spaghetti bubbling in a kitchen pot like the entrails of a small animal. I pictured Kim Sutton arriving with a bottle of inferior Côtes du Rhône for her inferior new boyfriend. Then Roland lit an incense stick, and I smelt it in Ireland. It turned out to be frankincense burning in a cemetery thurible.

After we put the coffin in the ground, they covered the hole with fake grass and crossed muddy shovels to show it was all over. Forever. I spent twenty minutes shaking hands with a long line of depressed overcoats. Men who looked like earwigs in belted gabardine and who smelt of prune juice, pipe tobacco and Power's whiskey.

"Sorry son... Awful tragedy... Loss... Loss... Grief... Sadness... Loss." I only heard words, not sentences. I shook their hands. They went away happy.

Niall drove me to the ferry in his respectable car, and we said goodbye while looking in opposite directions. I needed to get back to London. Ireland was already empty and there was a blank space in my head where home used to be.

The harbour horn sounded and the water hurled itself against the hull. The ship dived between the waves like a moaning, rusting whale and the Dún Laoghaire streetlights disappeared behind a screen of spray. I checked my wallet. Twenty-six pounds. Sterling. Ugly money with the Queen looking at you sideways, as though you'd pushed in beside her on a bus seat. I went below to the heaving car deck and rolled an unsteady joint, a mangled stalk of paper and spit fabricated in a dark, diesel-slicked corner. I thought about Kim Sutton, and I knew she too was lost.

Two days earlier, she had kissed me sweetly in Euston station. She'd given me a copy of the *Evening News* and a packet of Fox's glacier mints before pressing herself against me for the last time. I'd watched her as the train pulled out and tried to open a window, but you can't do that anymore. You can't touch the fingers you love. Something to do with air conditioning.

She had disappeared quickly. The train rumbled and then swerved through grey sunlight and back yards full of wreckage. I sucked on a Fox's glacier mint, and watched London as it thinned out into long, streaky suburbs where women struggled with prams and shopping bags, like pack mules in headscarves.

In Holyhead harbour, the North Wales police, all cheap suits and droopy moustaches, swarm around the young male immigrants like bees about a honey jar. So many to choose from and so

3

little jail space. "All right, sir. If you wouldn't mind stepping this way, sir. Over here, sir." It's a competition to see who can put the most "sirs" in a sentence, yet remain hostile.

"For what reason?" I ask.

"Reason, sir? I don't need a reason."

I mention that I might miss the train to London.

"Sir, please step into the booth, sir, now!"

Inside the booth, there's a desk with a ballpoint pen and a piece of paper. It's the Prevention of Terrorism Act. I sign it, and a moustache curls upwards in a smile.

On the platform I approach a uniformed man with a whistle and a hearing aid. "Is this the 6:55 to Auschwitz?" I ask.

"Enough of your cheek, lad."

"*Arbeit macht frei!*"

"What?"

"It's Gaelic for thank you."

"Thank you too. Now get aboard or we'll leave without you."

The ashtrays overflow and the seats reek of Paddy sweat mixed with cement dust. The heating doesn't work and the floor is sticky. The luggage racks sag, and there is no buffet service, because God only knows what demented energy might be awakened if they actually fed us.

The track rattles, passengers shake in their sleep, until BOOM! London. Honey, I'm home.

Roland is extremely surprised when he opens the door and finds me standing there. "Hey, Barry! Sorry to hear about your mum."

I nod. Inside the house, a floorboard creaks.

"Mind if I come in?"

He looks back over his shoulder, nervously, and then says in a loud, deliberate voice, "Sure. Come on in, BARRY!"

Roland walks in front of me. He has a nice arse, as men's arses go. I picture Kim Sutton kissing it, and then I picture Roland kissing it. He teaches yoga, so it is conceivable. We pass the kitchen and I notice two plates, freshly daubed with spaghetti sauce, soaking in a blue basin in the sink. The floorboard creaks again. The evidence is mounting.

Into the living room we go, with its Pink Floyd pyramid poster and cat-scratched stereo speakers. Roland falls back into a corduroy beanbag so soft it could sap his soul, if he had a soul.

"Like to do a line?" he asks.

"Why not?"

Roland chops out two fine lines of amphetamine sulphate, and this gets me thinking. If he knows why I'm here – if he is concealing my girlfriend in a bedroom upstairs – if he has heard the rumours concerning my extremely volatile temper – then what the fuck is he doing giving me something that's only going to make me angrier? I offer him my last Fox's glacier mint. He looks puzzled as he refuses. Upstairs, now there is only silence.

He snorts his line. Then I snort mine.

"So what brings you here?"

I tell him I'm just killing time and he drifts off into some nervous chit-chat that washes over me. I switch him off, but his lips continue to move. Maybe it's the tiredness. I haven't slept in such a long time. I keep promising myself some rest, but then I think, *You'll have all the time in the world to sleep when you're 30.*

I know that back home, Niall is going through the cardboard boxes laden with her possessions. He's putting to one side anything that looks vaguely official. He'll pay all her bills. Death, after all, is no excuse for a lapse in financial propriety. Anything personal he will carefully save in a box marked "Personal Effects". This will include the plain postcards I have sent her. He will read

5

each one with a look of bafflement on his face. My jokes about the English and their love for whippets, bingo and garden ornaments will strike him as mean-spirited and ungracious. He will place my cards at the bottom of the box and cover them with dry-cleaning receipts and invoices for minor household repairs, like a dog burying an unpleasant mess.

I look at Roland.

"Are you all right?" he asks.

"Right enough for another line," I reply.

He is not happy about sharing his gear with a chap who might turn homicidal at any minute. He's older, sure enough, but I'm bigger and Irisher and yoga is not a martial art. It's fine for premenstrual tension, but it's not going to stop a Doc Martens.

He chops up two more lines then offers me the fatter of the pair. I lean forward, wink at him and then, with total disregard for druggie protocol, I snort both of them. I'm vaguely aware of his astonishment. "Mind if I use your bathroom?" I ask, but I'm already on my feet, marching towards the staircase. I pounce up the steps, two at a time. In the bathroom, I turn on the cold tap and watch it trickle and curl in the green-stained basin. Even the water in this house is grubby.

I flush the toilet and walk out the door. At the bottom of the stairs Roland stands, a look of pure nausea spreading across his mangy features. I walk towards the bedroom. The door is half-open and there is a light glowing on the other side. I know. I definitely know. She's in there, coiled fearfully on a bed, waiting for a world of anger to explode. She has seen me in full flight. She has witnessed the wreckage: furniture upended, windows smashed, ornamentation stomped, mirrors fragmented. I don't hurt people, but I'm hard on fixtures and fittings.

Roland shouts up the stairs: "Barry! Wozzup, mate? Oi!"

6

I push the door. The hinges squeak. I look down the stairs at this man who has unwittingly shared with me the last of his speed. He looks up at me, the man who has unwittingly shared the last of his girlfriend. There is nothing between us but air and light and time.

Time.

I'll read this again someday. Perhaps I'm reading it now. Maybe it's 1989 and I'm thirty. I've lost half my hair and my belly is pressing against my belt. Or who knows, could it be that it's 1999 and I'm forty? Older than Jesus. Older than Joplin. Fifty or even fucking sixty years old? I don't think so. The future doesn't stretch that far.

If anybody is reading this in 2019, it's you, Niall, isn't it? You're settling my affairs, paying my bills, and arranging for Cousin Phil, deaf and breathless, to give the final bagpipe lament. Perhaps you see reading my diary as a familial duty. Getting to know your younger brother now that he's safely dead. Maybe you're even reading it for the second time. If so, you already know that I stand for a long time at that half-open door, Kim Sutton on the other side. You've already watched me lumber down the stairs, push Roland to one side and step out into the cold, Kennington night. You've seen me hop a night bus for Brixton, where the bad boys on the front line are selling uncut energy wrapped in neatly folded paper. Two snorts on Coldharbour Lane and I turn into Super Paddy, the conflicted comic book hero who doesn't know whether to fly, cry or sing "The Fields of Athenry".

I'm sure you tut-tutted at the moment where I run headlong and headstrong across Vauxhall Bridge, throwing jacket, shirt and shoes into the river. You're shocked, but you're exhilarated. Read on.

2

JOB

MONDAY, MARCH 5, 1979

I pound a fist on the drawing board, and startle half the office.
I don't know what I'm doing here. I'm surrounded by skilled
architects, structural engineers and designers. I am an island of
incompetence in an ocean of technical talent.

Dave Rennie stands at the desk beside me. He is a 28-year-old
Londoner with a mass of draughting experience. A little while
ago, he leaned across the gap between our desks and asked, with
genuine curiosity, "How did you ever get this job?"

"Simple," I said. "The man who hired me is trying to fuck me."

Dave Rennie laughed, but a pain shot through his heart. He
is not a handsome young man like yours truly and therefore has
no option but to rely on his ability. And, as everybody knows,
ability fades.

Two months ago, I came to this office on the Uxbridge Road
for an interview with the project manager. Mr Longley wore a
loose wedding ring that slid back and forth on his finger like a

bead on an abacus. When he reclined in his swivel chair, his neck disappeared into the striped material that was part shirt, part optical illusion. He looked up from his notes, and was clearly surprised by my youth.

"Oh!" he said, eyes dragging over my body like a stoker's rake. "You're quite... splendid. Please do sit down."

I found my attention drifting towards a framed photo on his desk. It showed a debonair and rascally gent with a spotted tie, trimmed moustache and a large toss of wavy hair. I wondered if it was his father, or else perhaps a lesser-known villain from Edwardian vaudeville.

Did I mention I was stoned?

"So, Barry," he said. "You have worked in the nuclear power industry before?"

"Yes," I replied, "I worked for a French uranium company, back in Ireland. Exploration, that sort of thing."

"*Parlez-vous français?*" He asked.

"*Oui,*" I responded nonchalantly. "*Un petit peu.*"

He was impressed, but he had just witnessed the usage of my entire French vocabulary.

"You are familiar with Calder Hall?"

"Calder Hall," I replied. "Yes, of course."

I pictured a great, stately pile occupied by Mr Toad. Nearby was a lake with Ratty and Mole in a rowing boat. I was incredibly stoned.

"We need somebody to oversee the decontamination systems at Calder Hall. In addition, there is a cladding maintenance issue – straightforward stuff, five-millimetre stainless steel. You've worked with that?"

"Absolutely," I replied, my teeth parting slightly to allow the giant lies to escape.

Then he moved off in a completely unpredicted direction. "I've never been to Ireland," he said. "A lot of British people are put off. The political thing, you know. Things are difficult."

I agreed. Things were difficult.

"You don't have any...?"

He was too polite to finish the question, but I shook my head anyway, assuming he was referring to evil paramilitary affiliations.

"No, no. I'm from the Republic," I said, as if that explained anything.

"Yes, yes," he nodded, with a combination of embarrassment and geographical confusion. "You're miles away."

"Miles," I echoed.

He decided to return to a more comfortable topic. "I should give you a little info about the company. What you see on this level is a little less than a third of our operations. We're spread over four floors in the building. Upstairs, engineering; downstairs, civil. We're the technical chaps. You're the second new man. Raymond over there joined us about four weeks ago. Wife left him. Messy, messy, messy business. You are not married, are you?"

"No," I said.

"I expect you have a girlfriend?"

"No," I said, thinking of Kim Sutton and Roland Nice-Arse squirming around in a knot of dirty sheets, their bodies slapping each other like wet rubber gloves, their party-parts slurping each other's juices. "No," I repeated. "I'm as free as the day I was born."

The temperature rose slightly in the cubicle. He stubbed out his half-smoked Rothmans and lit another. We had a moment of silence as he searched for words to cover his desire.

"We'll soon be changing the project name," he said, "but it's just a PR exercise. Around here we'll continue to call it Windscale."

A mushroom cloud parted inside my head. The recruitment

agency had said very little about the job. They'd simply referred to it as a "prestigious life-changing opportunity". They had entirely forgotten to mention the giant outlet pipe that crapped, like Godzilla's arse, great radioactive turds into the Irish Sea.

"Sellafield will be the new name."

"Sellafield," I said, nodding my approval. Sell-A-Field. It sounded so harmless, like something a farmer might do if he were strapped for cash.

Mr Longley continued to talk, but my mind was elsewhere. I had a mental image of a giant atomic shockwave blasting across the ocean, picking up trawlers and ferries, flinging saltwater and mackerel into the heart of the Irish midlands. I pictured drowned cats and floating coffins, pulled from the soil like loose fencing pickets. I watched partially fried dogs yelping on half-submerged rooftops while men and women, as ragged as their migrant forebears, crawled with exhaustion onto islands of bobbing debris. I saw a perfect globe of brilliant light, flashing like hot magnesium, eating up all the colours in the world, swallowing everything, even shadow. Only a moral dwarf would even consider accepting a job like this.

"What's the salary?" I asked brightly.

"Starting at £14,000 a year, and please call me Chris."

A cluster of amphetamine crystals dissolved inside my head like temporal-lobe popcorn. My eyes opened wide and sparkled and a grin flashed on like a spotlight. Mr Longley seemed to interpret this behaviour as a small flirtation. He lost his way with words and grasped at the first notion that drifted into reach.

"I g-g-go to the theatre, sometimes," he stuttered. "The West End. It's rather fabulous."

This harmless statement came to my ears, deciphered and translated. "Are you interested in sodomy?" it said.

I said yes, yes, I was. I liked it very much, though I admitted that I'd grown up in a small town and we didn't have a whole lot of it. Theatre that is, I couldn't be sure about the sodomy.

"There's nothing quite as wonderful as live theatre," he said.

I nodded with enthusiasm, keeping a lid on my opinion that theatre was nothing but fat people in wigs with loud voices. Or was that opera?

"We must go sometime," he said. "Together."

"Oh yes," I replied. "We must."

Meanwhile, the amphetamine pixies pulled back the skin on my cheeks and gave me an expression of deranged curiosity. I imagined I looked like a barracuda in a wind tunnel. Chris Longley found himself matching my intensity of speech. He asked me a flurry of questions about my home life in Ireland. Was I enjoying London? How long had I been here? I told him only a week, and he trilled, "A week! Oh my goodness, you are seeing everything through such new eyes, new eyes!" He stared into my new blue eyes and transmitted a bright red laser of lust. "Still, I'm sure you were upset leaving home."

I left home on a Sunday night. The platform was clotted with Sparrow Mammies, tiny women who peck at their children, mostly girls in striped UCD scarves.

Smoke and jostling filled the carriages. Three men in crumpled suits, who looked like they had spent a losing day at the races, drank small bottles of Guinness. A folded newspaper with an abandoned crossword rested on the table between them. People coughed, for fear that silence might take hold.

Athy... Newbridge... Kildare...

We picked up speed, then stopped just as suddenly. Doors opened and slammed shut as more excited students climbed aboard, heading for their cold-water bedsits with the barred basement windows, mildew-speckled ceilings and the bathtubs discoloured with oxidised swirls. The poverty of rural Ireland swept past the windows in a dun-coloured diorama of decay, pockmarked with abandoned rusty tractors and unpainted bungalows where men in dirty shirts plotted suicide by hanging from a rafter.

No. I did not feel sadness for all that I'd left behind.

"I have to ask you about secrets," said Chris Longley, regaining his composure. His words were mysteriously hushed.

"Secrets?" I replied, wondering if he was about to quiz me on my dismal academic results or the bank loan I'd never repaid. Prompted by my blank expression, he slid a printed sheet of paper across the desk.

"*Official* Secrets," he said.

The page was a bad photocopy and the words bled together like melted wax. The large print at the top of the page referred to the "1920 Act". Chris Longley unscrewed a fountain pen and I signed without bothering to decipher the molten gibberish.

"I think you will be happy here," he said.

I looked into his eyes and said yes, I thought I would be very happy.

He pointed to the dapper gent in the framed photograph on his desk. "Tom Tuohy," he explained. "Your fellow countryman... Well, he was born in the UK to Irish parents... A personal hero of mine."

He went on to tell me the *Tale of Tom Tuohy* in all its detail. It was a story so outrageously crazy that only a Paddy could be at its centre.

During the great Windscale fire of 1957, when it looked like the whole place was going up in smoke, Site Manager Tuohy was the man who'd saved the day. He had pulled on his protective gear, climbed the burning reactor and peered into its very heart. He'd listened to its breath as it sucked in air from every corridor. He had patted its heaving hungry belly and then made the decision to shut off the cooling fans and pump in thousands of gallons of water.

"Outrageous!" exclaimed Chris Longley. "This was eleven tons of uranium, burning at over 1,000 degrees Celsius. The concrete shielding was withering under the extreme heat. As you know, molten metal causes water to oxidise. Hydrogen, explosive hydrogen, expanding into every nook of the cauldron! Tom Tuohy ordered the evacuation of the building, except for himself and his fire chief. Then he turned on the hoses, and miraculously the inferno was extinguished."

Chris Longley took out a handkerchief and dabbed his cheeks, which were now quite rosy, as though he too had been standing close to the flames. He was breathless as he asked me, straight up, whether I thought I could fill Tom Tuohy's radioactive shoes, and without the slightest hesitation I said, "Yes, sir."

He looked into my core, past the smouldering amphetamine fire, through the pressurised cloud of unshakable confidence and into the fast-breeding madness of a 20-year-old who was ready, willing and able to light a fuse and burn up the world. We shook hands. I turned and left Chris Longley's office, sensing that his eyes were all over me, but I didn't care. I now had something special, something almost beyond belief. I had something that half of Ireland would kill for.

I had a job.

GLOW

I could never get Kim Sutton to dress the way I wanted. She liked Laura Ashley. I wanted to track down Laura Ashley with a dog pack and beat her to death with a bolt of printed linen. Kim Sutton also liked blazers and polo-neck sweaters, shirts with collars that turned into bibs, pants with zippers on the side, suede boots and plaid tennis shoes. We had our first argument when I said, "I don't mind you dressing like one of Charlie's Angels, but does it have to be Kate fucking Jackson?"

The year before we left home, I was interviewed for a job at *Energie Nouvelle,* a French mining company prospecting for uranium on the slopes of Mount Leinster. Outside on the street, a herd of hippies walked in circles. Christy Moore, the sweaty conscience of Ireland, had started singing anti-nuke songs, and the festival at Carnsore Point had rallied the raggedy hordes who wanted their electricity generated by chicken farts and copper wire wrapped around potatoes. Everywhere you went you saw the dopey smiling sun logo and the words *Atomkraft nein danke!* Nobody else in town had applied for the position.

The chants of "No atoms here!" drifted in through the open window, causing my interviewers, François and Alain, to shift nervously. A local man, Benny Hennessy, had been appointed in the role of translator, even though the entire interview was being conducted in English.

"Benny," said François. "Tell him the job has some hazards."

"The job," said Benny, "has some hazards."

"But it also has some benefits," said Alain.

"There's good stuff too," said Benny.

"You will receive local holidays," said François. "But we also recognise Bastille Day and November Eleven."

"That's more time off than you were expecting," said Benny.

"Punctuality is important to us," said Alain.

"Just get out of the bed in the morning," said Benny.

"There is a two-week trial period," said François.

"Any arsing around and you're out," said Benny.

"You may find yourself some distance from town, and we do not make specific provisions for lunch," said Alain.

"Bring sandwiches," said Benny.

Later that day, I met Kim Sutton on the bridge in the middle of the Rainy Town. She asked me if I had gotten the job. "*Bien sûr*," I said. She wore a yellow dress with frilly sleeves that came as far as her elbows, and there was a large white bow at her neck. I told her she looked like one of the medieval waitresses they laid on for the tourists at Bunratty Castle.

"Exactly how would you like me to dress?" she asked.

"Well," I said. "You have Debbie Harry's high cheekbones, full lips and everything. Maybe you could dress a bit more like her?"

Sometimes, when you wrap a request in a compliment, it works. I had a mental picture of Debbie Harry in leather jeans, studded belt and a sheer nylon top with black bra visible beneath. Kim Sutton looked right through me, into the horny emptiness, and said, "Right," but when the word "right" is divided into two syllables, it's rarely a sign of compliance.

I reminded her that we were going to see The Radiators from Space playing in La Plaza later that week. There'd be a rough crowd, I expected.

"Meaning?" she asked.

"Meaning you could end up swinging by that bow, if you're not careful." I tried to make it sound light-hearted and humorous. It came across hostile.

I started work the following morning. François gave Benny instructions, and Benny passed them on to me. "You'll have three young lads with you," said Benny. He nodded at the sullen youths who stood in the yard smoking Major cigarettes and cursing. "We hired them from the special school as a goodwill gesture to the community, but they're total fucking nut jobs. Just try and stop them from doing any damage."

So this was to be my career: chaperone to three juvenile delinquents, Donal, Ulick and Maurice, or as I came to call them collectively, DUM. I piled them into the back of a white Renault 6 and as we drove out onto River Street, they hurled abuse at the protesting hippies.

"We're gonna nuke yiz."

"Atomkraft nein wank!"

"Pluton-i-um, up yer bum."

We travelled out along the Black Bog Road until we came to the drilling rig, a flatbed truck with a tower on the back. A long-haired man called Tommy operated the rig. He had smoke-yellow fingers and the smell of hash oil leached from his pores.

He stamped a muddy boot when DUM got out of the car. "Keep those cunts away from the rig," he said. "Last time they were here they fucked up everything."

I helped Tommy load boxes of core into the back of the car as DUM bounced crab apples off each other's heads. When the car was fully loaded, we took off for Site A, a bumpy ride further up the mountain. Small red flags marked the fields and we drilled beside each one with a hand auger. Between flags, DUM chased each other with nettles, leaving red welts on faces and hands. When I told them to knock it off, they imitated my accent and pranced around the field in a girlish fashion. They ate their lunch in a lean-to shed and then tried to set fire to a bale of straw. It was too damp to burn, so they cursed and smoked Major cigarettes.

The next couple of hours we spent cleaning out a riverside warehouse that had once belonged to the Health Board. It was to be our "centre of operations" but it smelled of antiseptic and sickness. DUM discovered several wheelchairs under a canvas sheet, which they raced around in circles, crashing into one another and then screaming "insurance claim!" as they rolled on the floor clutching an arm or a leg.

I went back to the rig to pick up another ten boxes of core, leaving DUM to their own devices. Tommy sat in the cab as the drilling pipe spun in the ground. The water pumped in and the sludge pumped out. He opened the passenger door and I sat in beside him; he didn't try to hide the fact he was smoking a joint. He passed it to me. The rain came down and the windscreen clouded over. "Where did you leave the loonies?" he asked.

I told him about the warehouse and he reckoned it would be burnt down before I got back.

"What do you think of the job?" he asked.

I tipped some ash off the joint and said, "I like it so far."

There was an eight-track stereo in the cab and Tommy pulled some tapes from under the seat. "Not my music," he said. "Country and Western. Belonged to the last guy."

It was mostly big hats from Ballymena and cotton-pickers from Cookestown, but we found a Jim Reeves in the middle. Welcome to my World crackled through the speaker as the pipe drill bottomed out behind us. Tommy told me about his father, a man he held in equal measures of fear and admiration.

The man had four rundown houses near the Regional College and he let them out to rat-like students. "He calls them 'rudents,'" said Tommy. "And he beats them up if they don't have the rent." He told me his father made a small fortune driving transcontinental trucks to the meat markets in Paris and the American bases between Wiesbaden and Stuttgart. "He used to bring back some savage porn. I saw one magazine called *Amputease* – Fellas and girls without arms and legs." Tommy shuddered and dropped the subject. I helped him add another pipe on the back of the rig and we watched it plunge into the dirt, fucking the earth beneath our feet. It felt like Tommy's troubled father was guiding our terrible thoughts – or maybe it was just the hash.

Benny was waiting for me at the warehouse. "Don't ever leave these bastards unattended again," he said. "I just fished three wheelchairs out of the river."

We laid out the granite core from the drilling rig on a series of folding tables and Benny closed most of the shutters. Three cigarettes glowed in the darkness and we could hear the mumbled cursing. Benny called DUM to the tables and he gave each man an ultraviolet lamp. "You have to scan this stuff," he said. "We're looking for 'fluorescent green.'"

He touched a sliver of Uranium-235 with one of the lamps and the room lit up in a burst of chartreuse. DUM picked up their lamps and scanned the core with an unusual level of enthusiasm. Murmurs of excitement and yelps of joy accompanied the occasional flashes of green.

"That was a big one."

"That was even bigger."

"That was the biggest."

Benny stood beside me and whispered, "They say overexposure to UV can lead to impotence, even sterility." As we listened to DUM "ooh" and "aah" in the darkness, we agreed that such an outcome might be for the best.

Later, I stood outside La Plaza waiting for Kim Sutton. La Plaza was a long, windowless tunnel, more suited to growing mushrooms than hosting musical events. The owner was a short, dapper man with a flop of chestnut hair and platform shoes with buckles. He focused most of his attention on his flirtatious wife, a woman who stared into your eyes as she pulled the Guinness, her delicate hand wrapped around the erect lever, squeezing a pint of sex into every half-pint glass. Her husband's eyes were everywhere she went. He hated the power of her body and the fact that her breasts sold half the tickets. If she spent too much time with a customer, he called her name or he pushed her aside and took over the task himself. He was so much more than a spouse; he was *coitus interruptus* in a double-breasted suit.

The La Plaza doors opened, and there was still no sign of Kim Sutton. I got up close to the front because I needed the noise the way a junkie needs junk. There was jostling and spilt drink, but no fists thrown. When you're in a small town with only one place to go, you can't afford to be banned for life. Without La Plaza, there is no life.

The band came onto the stage and tore into *Blitzin' at the*

Ritz and followed it with *Sunday World*. Leather slapped against leather like jostling cattle on a slaughterhouse floor. Steve Rapid and Philip Chevron came down into the crowd. The Telecaster flashed and the microphone cable snaked around us. This band was our Damned, our Clash, if Joe Strummer had read Joyce and Brian James had listened to Weill.

A photographer with a press badge circled the crowd with a wide-angle lens. The floor shook and the tables trembled. The reason old people don't like punk is partly because of the way it rearranges the furniture. I got up and started to pogo with fifty other lunatics, I had two bumps of speed, four pints of Harp and *Television Screen* blasting from the speakers. Nothing could pull out the pegs and take me down. And then Kim Sutton walked in.

"Did you dress that way on a dare?" might be one of the meanest expressions in Ireland, but those were the words that sprang to mind. She slid between the tables in an ecru dress with puffy shoulders and choker collar. She wore pale blue tights and a pair of slingback huarache sandals. Capping it off, in every sense, was the circle of daisies in her hair. Actual fucking daisies. She took a seat close to the front and though the band didn't exactly stop, the tempo clearly shifted from allegro to adagio. She sat down, primly, on the edge of a stool and watched the stage like an attentive school-girl studying algebra on a blackboard. She was Mary Poppins in a Breughel painting, Saint Bernadette in a Marseille whorehouse. The flash flashed and the camera snapped.

Two days later, our finest national newspaper printed a picture from the gig. One picture, that was all. The band was somewhere out of sight and the focus was on the audience, the grotesque twisted mascara and spit-dripping lips, the gnashing teeth and the cold sweat gathered around staring eyeballs. In the foreground, illuminated by invisible light, her hair tossed by the softly blown breath of cherubs – a young woman with daisies in her hair. The caption was "A Pearl Before Swine".

I folded the paper and made a promise – a pact with my future self. Someday I would hunt down Laura Ashley, and push her down the stairs.

4

MUSIQUE

SATURDAY, MARCH 1, 1979

Kevin and I stand in the Young Ireland Ballroom and study the strange, gyrating creatures. There is nothing remotely attractive in the posturing and prancing and posing, but that doesn't matter because we haven't come here for the dancing. Nor have we come to pick up heavy girls and transport them into a state of blissful matrimony. We're certainly not here for the music. We are looking for one particular in-bred face in a vast sea of many.

"One, two and a one-two-three," says the Queen of Irish Country Music as she drops the microphone stand to its lowest notch. She wears a sequinned jacket with a collar so big it looks like someone has tried to slice off her head with a boomerang.

"Testing, testing, testing..."

The dancehall in Harlesden is run by a pea-faced priest called Father Hegarty. A breeder of hard-working man-horses, he pokes and prods his sires into action on Friday and Saturday nights. The whole romantic enterprise is based on the fact that half the

Paddies in London hope to marry a fat little nurse from Mayo, a flush-cheeked, bosomy creature with a forgiving nature and a functional knowledge of fellatio. It's more grapple than dance, with men and women drunkenly whirling about the floor like items of clothing in a tumble dryer.

The Queen of Irish Country Music stands in front of an old slide projection of an Irish street scene, circa 1950: a retarded population, scared in equal measure by God and fashion, their clothes made from rags dipped in bog water, their cars the mechanical biscuit tins inherited from the English: Morris Cowleys, assorted Cambridges and Rileys, and the never-faithful Austin 10.

What do you call a British car owner? A fucking pedestrian.

Kevin and I find what we're looking for. We both focus on the same ugly, misshapen man on the other side of the dance-floor. Mandy McKenna is not a pretty sight. He has pork-chop ears and a beak for a nose. He's the brother you prefer not to talk about, the uncle you rarely see, the child you hope you never have. He is the foetus that somehow made it past the coat-hanger. He nods at us and we step out onto the worn maple floor where most of his business transactions take place.

Her Royal Highness, the Queen of Twang, tightens the knob on the microphone stand, then snaps her fingers with an amplified clickety-clack. The band prances onto the stage, all indigo costumes and fat, calloused hands. They look less like musicians and more like the stokers on some queer cruise ship. Some old spit is drained from the water key on the alto sax and a mewling tone is pulled from the sagging lung of a button accordion.

"How'ya?" roars the Queen.

"Grand!" the crowd roars back.

If you thought the worse thing the Irish ever did to London

was put a bomb in Harrods, then you've never heard *Mary McCrory's Mistical Men*, or *Danny Driscoll and his Mullingar Moonshiners* or *Chipper O'Neill and the Boys from the Barracks* as they gang-rape the Nashville songbook.

"Testing, testing one-two-three."

Mandy's moniker comes from the Irish tradition of calling a man after his chosen profession. Mandy is a retailer of Mandrax pills: what the Sun newspaper refers to as "Randy Mandies" and the Americans call "Quaaludes". He sells them for a quid apiece.

We wade through the roughnecks in their Bri-nylon shirts, and push through the stench of Brylcreem Original that hangs in the air like Zyklon-B.

"Testing, testing seven-eight-nine."

We cut deeper through the crowd, into the ugly heart of the mob, where a fight is most likely to start.

"Well, lads," Mandy says when we come face-to-face, "Well, well, well, well, well." He is a fountain of wells. Money is handed over, and Mandy yells through cupped hands, "You'll have to go and see Paudie now. Paudie has the gear. You know Paudie, don't yiz?"

Everyone knows Paudie. Paudie hails from somewhere deep in County Roscommon where they make pies out of sick children. He talks through a scattering of crooked teeth and his words come out in short, mangled sentences.

Mandy disappears into a hedgerow of corduroy jackets and shiny-arsed gabardine pants. Kevin pushes forward until he too is swallowed, but I find my path blocked by a giant in a dung-coloured three-piece suit. The monster wears a necktie with a knot the size of a clenched fist. His clenched fists are the size of bowling balls. The only reason he has developed opposable thumbs is because he needs them to operate a shovel.

"Excuse me," I say, but the monster refuses to budge.

"Wha' are you doing here?" bellows the monster, and it's a reasonable question because I don't look like I belong anywhere. Ramones jeans, sharkskin jacket and a T-shirt that reads "Heroin Only Kills The Weak". My hair is spiked and prickly to the touch, my eyes darkened by sleepless nights and bad romantic judgment. Oh yes, and I'm carrying a knife.

A tortured note rings out from the stage and the three-piece drum kit kicks into life. *Kish-Kish*, goes the hi-hat.

"I asked ya' a question," says the monster.

The bass guitar climbs to the cruising altitude where it will remain for the rest of the night, repeating the exact same phrase, something that sounds like the words *Humpty-Dumpty, Humpty-Dumpty*, over and over again.

Kish-Kish... Humpty-Dumpty... Kish-Kish.

The Queen of Irish Country Music starts to sing and her Donegal accent creeps through the air, a dissonant flatulence gassing a song that has four words, three chords, and no earthly reason for existence.

"I'm not goin' to ask you again."

I look up into the eyes of this side-burned, sociopathic sisterfucker. I see a walnut-sized brain and a 40-watt bulb with one illuminated thought: *when the band starts playin', the fightin' starts*. For a moment I feel a twinge of sorrow, not for the monster and the terrible tragedy that is about to befall him, but for the loss of my own musical youth.

Punk music is dead. The anthems can now be heard only after midnight, radio echoes, zombie love-calls rippled with static: the opening scream of "Neat, Neat, Neat" mixed with the broken-china-cup piano of "Piss Factory"; white noise rising over the airways and disappearing into the darkness of time. Punk is dead

and yet this shite is alive. Out with t/
There is no justice in the World of S/

"Answer me!" roars the monste
bowling-ball fist. Some frothy sal/
a dangling, liquid question marl
curiosity.

Kish-Kish... Humpty-Dumpty...

The din gnaws into my head like a hungry rat. ı t.....
chip shop in Wood Green and the juke box full of "Rock Classics"
– Johann Sebastian Zeppelin and Ludwig Van Bachman-Turner
Overdrive – and the little Greek girl behind the counter who
uses the phrase "my love" in every single sentence, in a soft voice
that sometimes gives me an erection.

"Would you like salt on that, my love?" – and then she dips
her delicate hand into the heated glass case that contains the
thick, juicy sausage of kings.

"A squirt of ketchup on your saveloy, my love?"

One day I might ask her out, but I've had very little exposure
to Greek women and I'm concerned about their apparent genetic
predisposition towards facial hair. One does not want to fall asleep
beside Melina Mercouri and wake up next to Freddy Mercury.

"I'm talkin' to YA!" howls the monster.

The crowd presses in and the knife sneaks out. It's an old
American Shur-Snap with a black tar handle and a sweet stiletto
blade, not yet extended.

I look into the shallow pool of the big man's knowledge. I see
a grey soup filled with Republican songs, rosaries and pictures
of Elvis Presley and Padre Pio. I see secret homosexual longings,
recipes for rasher sandwiches and Gaelic football scores since
'62. Last, but by no means least, I see the list of fake names used
in different labour exchanges in pursuit of fraudulent claims.

sh... Humpty-Dumpty... Kish-Kish.

ss the button and the blade swings out, a sharp secret
en by the passing movement of bodies. The monster's belly
ooks like a laundry sack filled with wet cement. It heaves, sways, and rolls from side to side. It rubs against a Rayon shirt, generating static, forcing short hairs out through buttonholes where they become charged tendrils, arcing and sparking against a belt buckle the size of a hubcap.

The monster opens his mouth to say something loud, noxious, and fearsome, but the words never come. Instead, his eyes turn to water, his knees bend and his shoulders fold in like butterfly wings. He descends into the quicksand of pain with a twisted face and quivering lips. He hits the ground with a sodden thump.

Kish-Kish... Humpty-Dumpty... Kish-Kish.

I am perplexed because the knife still hangs at my side, bright and shining and clean as a whistle. The belly of the beast is still intact with no guts, no gore spilled on the floor.

Something else entirely has brought about the dramatic collapse of Goliath. A steel-tipped boot has cut through the chancers and dancers and slammed into the monster's shin, crushing it like a one-stem vase caught in the path of a ball-peen hammer. The boot belongs to Kevin. His face bobs into view, bright, tight, and energized.

The call goes out: "Somebody bashed Dinny!"

"Tell Danny, somebody bashed Dinny."

A woman screams. A glass shatters.

"Who bashed Dinny?"

The crowd searches itself for the enemy within: the basher of Dinny. Bouncers take to the floor, four abreast, like minesweepers. Father Hegarty, his bald head speckled with rainbow dots from the mirror ball, puts down a bottle of warm 7up, rolls up his black sleeves and wades into the mayhem.

Kevin's hand reaches out and drags me through an opening in the swirling chaos.

Paudie leans against a column, not even vaguely interested in the war raging all around him. When he sees us approach, he pulls a plastic bag from his pocket. "Quare sport, the fuck," he says, making sense only to himself. His hand touches Kevin's hand, and the deal is done with speed, accuracy, and near-invisibility.

We head for the exit. The Queen of Irish Country Music croons a tale of happy girlhood spent in buttercup pastures into the vortex of raging testosterone. The accordion player steps nervously back from the edge of the stage. The drummer scrunches up and makes himself a smaller target for flying bottles.

Kish-Kish... Humpty-Dumpty... Kish-Kish.

We reach the door without further adventure and, just as we hit the fresh outside air, a young lady arrives. She's the original of the species, the puffy little full-breasted Mayo nurse herself, all handbag and hairspray and hope. When she sees two young men departing, two fine catches, she moans in abject disappointment. She watches us go, into the black London night, and her voice is small and helpless, the words almost lost in the racket and riot coming from inside the ballroom.

"Ah lads, you're not leaving already?"

5

LOVE

We walked up Seven Sisters Road in a small narcotic cloud, our voices booming like foghorns in the empty night. We talked about my broken relationship with Kim Sutton, and Kevin said, "The reason women live longer than men is because murderers tend to outlive their victims." He really knew how to cheer me up. I changed the topic, and we ended up discussing Amy.

"Amy," said Kevin.

It was a beautiful name. Back in Ireland, there were no Amys, just Miriams. The country was full of Miriams. You couldn't walk fifty yards without bumping into one.

"Amy was posh and beautiful and clever," he said, sucking the life from a joint. "She was pale and blonde with an upper-class lisp."

A speech impediment in Britain is often the sign of high breeding. In Ireland, it's usually the result of in-breeding. Dirt in the blood, mud on the vocal cords.

"I worked for her older sister, Louise," he said. "Built her kitchen extension in Maida Vale."

The whole thing was weird. Kevin never talked about love or sex.

"Louise and me, we were just friends," he said. "You know the way it is."

I didn't.

"One day she says, 'I'm bringing you to my parents' house. There's someone I want you to meet.'"

After work, Louise drove him to a smart suburb and a home with a rambling garden and silk curtains rippling in the windows. Inside the house, it was all parquet and wax polish, aspidistras perched on pot stands and a newel post with a bronze ballet dancer juggling a globe of light.

"Class."

"Yeah."

Louise led Kevin into a parlour, then withdrew. A beam of sunshine burned through a gap in the silk and illuminated Amy. Kevin had never seen anyone so lovely. She patted the sofa and he sat down beside her. They talked about everything. She asked about his childhood in Ireland and he told her he'd grown up in a castle, a lie so monstrous it had its own atmosphere. He asked her if she would like to go for a walk and she said yes.

"And then," he said, "you won't believe what she pulled out from beside her armchair."

Kevin's expression told me it was something obscene or preposterous. Maybe a top hat and a set of steak knives, a ukulele and a kilo of gruyère, a bust of Elvis Presley... When you're stoned, it's difficult to spot the rhetorical.

"A wheelchair," said Kevin, and then he went very quiet.

What was she doing with a wheelchair? Perhaps Amy was a nurse and this was a tool of her trade? Or she was an actress and this was a prop? Or she'd found it at the side of the road and she would put a small ad in the Lost & Found?

"Don't you get it?" said Kevin. "Amy was paralysed. From the waist down."

A cab squeaked past on the wet road. An arm stuck out through a passenger window and waved a golf club.

"Fore!" shouted a voice from within. The driver barked and the club disappeared. The window wound up and the night returned to quiet except for the sound of our lazy footsteps.

"She was still beautiful." Kevin's voice choked.

"You were in love?"

"Yeah."

Here was a first in the history of North London: two Paddies openly discussing their emotions. When it comes to matters of the heart, the Irish usually express their feelings through violence. If we fancy you, we break a chair. Totally smitten? We throw a car battery off an overpass into speeding traffic. This was uncharted territory.

"So I got behind the wheelchair and took Amy for a walk. We came to this little wooded area, bone-dry in the summer heat. We were both doing acid. Did I mention that?"

"No you did not."

"When she spoke," he said, "the words came out of her mouth in a ribbon, like a ticker tape, and it was all in capital letters."

"What did it say?"

"It said WOULD-YOU-LIKE-TO-FUCK-ME?"

"You're joking."

"I'm not. I checked it twice."

"Maybe you made a mistake," I said earnestly. "Maybe it was a typo."

But there was no mistake. She wanted him there and then. He

took her out of the chair and laid her down on the warm, dry grass. He ran his lips along the side of her cheek. He kissed her neck. He kissed her fingertips. He took off her clothes.

Sheltered by nature, he propped her against a tree. Branches swayed. Ripened acorns fell from above, bouncing off their heads in an erotic variation of the Isaac Newton tableau.

A Persian woman with dark, downcast eyes and a loose headscarf rushed past us. There was a moment of perfume, sandalwood, maybe furniture polish. She stopped outside a second-hand shop and looked in the window at a small electronic piano, priced fifteen pounds. She threw a glance backwards, and moved on.

"Where was I?" asked Kevin.

"Having sex with Amy."

"Yeah. I was sucking her toes."

Here was a side of Kevin rarely seen. By day, a humble bricklayer in Maida Vale; by night, a ravenous toe-sucker.

"She tasted like honey. Her feet were virginal, you know what I'm saying? Most feet get worn down, hurt, hobbled by bad shoes, corns, bunions and in-grown toenails, but not these. I was into these feet. I stroked them. I massaged them. I squeezed them. I studied them close-up. I brushed them against my cheek. I talked to them."

"You talked to her feet?"

"Yeah."

"What do you say to a foot?"

"Same stuff you say to a breast. You never did that?"

I had to admit that when it came to a woman's body parts I wasn't a great conversationalist.

"You don't talk to women during sex?"

The truth was I barely spoke to them beforehand.

The Persian woman stopped to look in another shop window.

"We did it," continued Kevin matter-of-factly, "for more than an hour, and then she ... You know." He made a gesture that could either have been a flower blossoming or a volcano exploding. He tapped the side of his head, "*This* is where the orgasm happens. It doesn't matter if the body is broken."

Never mind the deadened nerves like tiny ice cubes, their tendrils frozen and incapable of carrying any neural information, their secret messages of joy forever trapped inside a cold prison, a literal cell. Amy was above science. The physical disability only added to her allure. She was worth a thousand Miriams.

"Afterwards, I dressed her," he said, as if it was the most normal post-coital act imaginable. "Have you ever dressed a woman?"

"No."

"Intimate," he said.

A bin lorry from the Borough of Haringey ratcheted past at ten miles per hour. The Persian woman was gone but the sandalwood remained. The outside of the world smelled like the inside of a church. Kevin took off, running. He caught up with the lorry and climbed onto the little platform at the back. He held out his hand.

"Come on. Jump aboard."

The lorry rumbled past Finsbury Park. The city was abandoned, the windows boarded up with silence.

"Tell me more about Amy."

But Amy was already gone and Kevin's mind raced ahead, playing with another dream, fabricating faces, dates and events. It was impossible to keep up with the population that multiplied inside his head. Kevin made people the way people made people, but without the sex, the waiting and the pain.

"What happened with Amy?"

Kevin smiled. "Did I tell you about the time I went to France on a trawler? Two nights at sea and waves as big as dancehalls."

"Amy!" I demanded, but Amy was gone and there was no chance she would ever return.

"The fog hung over the English Channel, pale and thick," he said, "like a big damp canvas tent. The fish jumped out of the water and landed on the deck, because they hated the sea, because the sea was crazy."

Kevin drifted into his world and I drifted into mine. Hash, Mandrax and fantasy fuelled the two of us. The lorry sped up on Seven Sisters Road.

"Who were the Seven Sisters?" I asked.

"THEY WERE TREES!" he shouted over the rattling bolts and hinges.

It sounded plausible, but with Kevin, you never knew for sure.

The pace of the truck was alarming and the potholes were many. We clung on.

"Where are we going?" I shouted.

"North!" Kevin shouted back.

We were two foolish Paddies, dumber than Harpo, hanging onto the back of a bin lorry, and we had no idea where we were going.

"I'm in love," I shouted at Kevin.

"With Amy?"

I shook my head and made a sweeping gesture that covered a ten-mile radius. I told him I was in love with the bin lorry and the dead flies stuck to its surface. I was in love with Persians and sandalwood polish; in love with the stars, the moon, and the night; in love with all seven Sisters and the Post Office tower that wobbled in the distant sky like a lanky kebab. I was in love with the Piccadilly Line and the 22 bus; in love with the chip shop in

Harlesden where patties nestled under glass like greasy museum exhibits; in love with the reggae that dripped from windowsills in Brixton and puddled on Railton Road. I was in love with the warm chocolate bars dispensed from tube station vending machines; in love with the waxy smell that came from Madame Tussauds. I was in love with everybody and everything and every moment in this great steaming pile of city.

The bin lorry shifted into warp speed and everything blurred around us. Kevin closed his eyes and thought about it all.

"Yeah," he said, his words half buried under a ton of noise. "Love!"

6

ART

I'm trying to figure out where it started to go wrong. Maybe it was the weekend we went to Winchester for the wedding of Kim Sutton's brother, Billy.

When we arrived at the train station, it was dark and late and there was nobody there to meet us. We rambled around for about an hour looking into every pub with livestock in the title: The Three Ducks, The Pig and Otter, The Olde Bull and the Farmer Fucking a Sheep. There was no sign of Billy and Irene. Kim Sutton looked at me nervously because she could feel the anger getting ready to spill.

"You're blaming me," she said.

"He's *your* brother."

The framed picture under my arm was getting heavier by the minute. She'd bought it on Oxford Street, in one of those shops that specialize in raping foreigners. It was of a young couple in silhouette running on a beach. They were naked, but the boy didn't appear to have any genitals.

"It's not my fault."

"If you just wanted me to haul something heavy through the streets," I said, "you should have bought me a big wooden cross."

"Now you're being a martyr."

Eventually we came to a place with a Watneys Red Barrel and through the leaded glass we could see Billy and Irene. They looked identical, with their long hippie hair and flat, dull expressions. Irene was from San Francisco and called everybody "guys".

"When did you guys get in?"

I felt like saying, "About a week ago, thanks to your fucking vague instructions," but Kim Sutton headed me off at the pass.

"We just got here. Here's our wedding present."

Irene pulled the brown paper from the picture and instantly started to sob. "It's sooooo beautiful. You guys are too much," she said. Then she hugged us both.

"Where did you get it?" Billy asked.

"Portobello Road," Kim Sutton lied.

"Wow, man. It's really authentic."

They propped it up on the bar counter and everybody in the place was forced to look at it.

Bert and Frieda, two of Billy's friends, dropped in and allowed me to buy them booze. They both drank cider. They both slurped. I hated their posture.

Nancy arrived a little before closing time. She was Kim Sutton's older sister, but I hadn't met her before. She spent her life drifting from commune to commune in Ireland and England, doing strange tribal stuff that she couldn't remember. She was the other side of the Kim Sutton coin. Instead of bright, fresh, strawberry blonde and healthy, Nancy was dark, bleak, curly and dangerous. She looked like an oversexed gypsy, someone who would take your hand, read it, and then sit on it.

"Little sister is doing all right," she said, taking me in from top to toe with great curiosity.

Kim Sutton looked away. She didn't often blush.

"What are you doing in London?" asked Nancy.

"I work for Armitage Shanks," I joked.

"Wow!" said Billy. "Don't they make the urinals?"

"Hand basins too," I said with wild enthusiasm. "Flush cisterns, bidets, vanity units..."

Nancy winked at me and said, "I think he's taking the piss."

When the pub closed, we headed back to the Billy-Abode, a two-bedroom flat that smelled of patchouli oil and damp dog. We sat around and smoked dope. Irene placed the wedding present on a mantle where it drew all conversation, its beauty expanding as the hours wore on.

"It's so trippy," said Billy.

"I think we know those guys," Irene pitched in, "They look like that couple who shared our tent."

"In Glastonbury?" asked Billy.

"Uh-huh. Remember we all got nude and danced in the rain?"

"I don't think it's the same couple," I said.

"What do you mean?" Irene said, pulling back her hair like a woman opening curtains.

"Guy in the picture doesn't have a cock," I said. "Did the guy in Glastonbury have a cock?"

Kim Sutton looked at the floor to cover her embarrassment. Irene wasn't happy. "What exactly are you?" she asked with a twist of sourness. "Some sort of cock expert?"

I leaned over very close to her face and replied, "Well, I do work for Armitage Shanks."

"Naughty boy," Nancy said, and then she laughed and slapped the back of my hand. She produced a ball of black gum and put it in a teapot lid. She struck four matches at once, and cooked it over a high flame. The smoke curled and twisted and we were lit up like tinkers around a campfire. We sucked in the fumes through a Biro tube until nothing mattered. Nothing mattered at all. Only smoke.

"You guys are sooo special," Irene said, and she started to sob again.

Bert and Frieda appeared to live in the flat next door, and yet they asked if they could crash for the night. Billy said, "Sure, man, no problem," and showed them to the second bedroom. I looked over at Kim Sutton and gave her my *what the fuck is this and where is our bed?* expression, but she was too stoned to notice.

Irene led their pet dog, a witless pooch called Sammy, out to a folded blanket in the kitchen. I was gob-smacked. "Even the fucking dog is getting his own room," I said, loud enough that even the mutt got the message.

We were given some cushions and a blanket. Nancy lay down on the sofa base beside us and covered herself with a shawl. Kim Sutton, as stoned as I'd ever seen her, crawled under the blanket on the floor and shut her eyes tightly.

The streetlight outside seeped in around the edges of the tie-dyed curtain.

"The room is going round," she said.

"That's what rooms are supposed to do," I replied.

She pressed herself against me in that state of demented horniness one gets at the apex of a buzz, when every part of the body becomes a sexual organ. I flipped open the top button on her jeans. "No," she whispered. "We're not alone."

I looked over her shoulder and said, "Nancy passed out ages ago."

Nancy smiled.

"Are you sure?" Kim Sutton asked, without opening her eyes.

"Certain," I whispered.

Nancy hovered like a wet shadow in the dark as she watched us fuck. She had a front-row seat in a sexual circus. Her features doubled in size as she moved closer to us. Her face loomed up over Kim Sutton's shoulders, and, for a brief glorious moment, it was almost like fucking a two-headed woman in the vastness of outer space.

Sammy the dog shuffled around in the kitchen. Kim Sutton dug her fingers into my back and imploded in a series of tight muscular seizures. Nancy gritted her teeth and rolled her eyes like a satisfied shark. It wasn't a three-way, but it was definitely a two-and-half-way.

I woke up a little before seven. Everyone was gone, except for the greasy neighbours. They were still in the second bedroom, fast asleep and wrapped around a pillow like snakes around a stick. They smelled as if they'd been sweating turpentine.

I woke up Kim Sutton.

"They're gone."

"Who's gone?"

"Billy and the blushing bride. What time is the ceremony?"

"I don't know, he didn't tell me."

"You didn't get an *RSVP, dude!* sort of thing"

Kim Sutton hated the hippie voice I used when imitating her brother. She dearly wanted to see her family as normal, but she was as close as they got to a straight arrow. She always had a job and never scrounged off the state. She believed that you could improve yourself, that you came into this world as raw material, to be shaped, formed and bettered.

About an hour passed, then the dog scratched on the door.

41

Irene entered wearing a small crown made from twisted wild flowers and twigs. She looked especially fucking stupid. Billy followed close behind.

"So," I said, "what time is this wedding?"

"That's all taken care of, man," Billy said.

"How do you mean *taken care of*?"

"We were up early, so we just got the sunrise ceremony out of the way."

I threw a glance at Kim Sutton and saw her look of alarm.

"We were going to wake you, man, but you looked so comfortable."

"Was it in a church?" I asked.

Billy laughed. "You couldn't see a sunrise in a church, man. No, it was on the top of the hill."

He got down and scrubbed Sammy's chin with his knuckles.

"Sammy had a great time, he woofed it up. You woofed it up, didn't you Sammy? You really woofed it up."

"It must have been good," I said. "If Sammy woofed it up."

"You really woofed it up, boy."

"What about Nancy?" I asked.

"Nancy went back to Brighton."

"Was she at the sunrise ceremony?"

"No man, she caught it last month."

"You did it last month as well?"

"We do it every month, man. You have to keep it fresh, you know?"

I didn't turn around and look at Kim Sutton, but I knew she was mortified. The whole journey had been nothing but a dumb waste of time.

On the Intercity back to London, I teased her relentlessly. "The bride said a few words, the groom said a few words and then Sammy woofed it up!"

Kim Sutton turned away and buried her head between the seat and the window.

"And then a passing sparrow made a speech, and a badger threw confetti..."

Kim Sutton twisted her head further away from me and began to shake. I was glad she was upset. I had lost a day's wages and we had made fools of ourselves. Never mind the forty quid we'd spent on the dickless boy on the beach.

"And then Sammy woofed it up again," I said.

The more her shoulders heaved, the better I felt. It was only right that she should pay with tears.

"Yeah, man, you gotta keep it fresh," I said.

Two weeks earlier, I had seen her face glow when she told me that Billy was getting married. It was a triumph of normalcy, the first step on the road to regularity. If Billy got married and Nancy gave up her gypsy wanderings and her sister Rosie stopped sleeping with men twenty years her senior... then all would be right with the world and Kim Sutton would be just like everybody else. I despised the aspiration for all its ordinary hope.

"The sunrise ceremony!" I spat.

When she tried to stifle her sobs, I knew it was mission accomplished. My hands were clean and now I could offer her comfort. I reached out and touched her shoulder.

"Hey," I said. "Hey, it's okay."

She turned to face me and I could see that she was laughing. Really laughing!

"Sammy woofed it up," she said, a smile bursting across her face.

In five seconds I went from stunned, to confused, to outraged, to angry, to almost happy. I never made her laugh. Never.

All the way back to London we took turns saying, "Sammy woofed it up," and the people around us picked up on it. An elderly man close by made a low bark and said, "Woof!" A woman with a purple umbrella said, "Woof, woof!" Another woman in a frayed anorak was even more adventurous: "Woof, woof, woofoooo!" she went.

I saw my reflection in the window. It didn't look as mean as it usually does, and though I knew it wouldn't last, I too allowed myself an ordinary dream. In it, I wasn't a monster. I didn't want to hurt people and bend them over until they snapped. I didn't have strange desires and wicked fantasies. With the right training, I could learn to be a proper boyfriend. Flowers, hugs and moonlit walks, that sort of shit – and once my spirit was broken, I might even pass as a husband.

Kim Sutton laughed and I laughed too, but we were laughing at different things. Four days later, she was in bed with another man.

7

FRANCE

I used to live in this house, so I still have a right to be here. I never returned the key, and if you keep the key, it's not breaking in.

Dermot MacMurrough stands in the hall, and he is totally freaking out. He has the look of a chicken on the chopping block, and yours truly is the farmer with the cleaver behind his back. He was talking merrily on the phone until I entered. "What are you doing here? You don't live here anymore!" he says. Clearly he is not familiar with the status conferred by key possession. "I'll call you back," he says into the receiver.

I walk to the end of the hall and put my key in the door of number two. I twist and twiddle, but it does not turn

"They changed the lock when your ex-girlfriend moved out."

"What do you mean, 'moved out'?"

"Two weeks ago."

Dermot MacMurrough does not like me. I once loaned him ten pounds, which he never refunded, so I bought a chain and locked his bicycle to the front fence, where it remains, deflated and rusting. Now it's payback time. Irish people will happily wait six or seven hundred years for a moment of revenge. Treachery is a national pastime, and when an Irishman offers you the hand of friendship, watch out for the kick in the bollocks.

"Where did she go?"

"I'm sure if she wanted you to know that, she would have told you."

Here you see in action Ireland's chief export to England: the cunt. We coddle and corn-feed them; we give them warmth, water and shelter; and then we put them on a boat and push them out into the Irish Sea.

"WHERE DID SHE GO?"

The heat of my question drives him back into a corner. "She went to France," he says.

I can't believe it. Why would she go to France? Who in their right mind goes to France?

"She took a job as an *au pair*, or a nanny. I don't know... Is there a difference?" He looks scared.

"Why, yes," I say, with two fingers touching a pensive chin. "The nanny is a childcare professional, not necessarily interested in cultural exchange. The *au pair*, on the other hand, is expected to fuck the kid's father." Then I turn and kick open the door.

"Hey! You can't do that."

"It's difficult, I admit, but not impossible."

I look around at a bedsit now cleaned beyond all recognition. Some powerful force has expunged the grime and the streaks of mildew, the cobwebs and the coal dust, the cigarette ash and the spider legs. This is no longer just a room; it is now a "room for rent", a place where the past has been erased with a mop and a bucket, where the future awaits its moment.

"You've got no right," Dermot MacMurrough says from beyond the door. "You have no right at all."

I had come halfway across London to demand and accept Kim Sutton's apologies. I'd expected raised voices and whimpers. Maybe a little sex. But France?

Fucking France.

Five years ago I'd been to Paris on a school tour.

"Oh wow! Look at the Eiffel Tower."

(Same as it looks on the biscuit tin.)

"Oh wow! The Mona Lisa."

(Same as the biscuit tin.)

Arc de Triomphe?

(Biscuit tin.)

It's an entire fucking city designed by McVitie's.

I look out the window we once looked out together, and I remember how our observations never matched. She saw a man with a dog; I saw a man with a hungry nuisance on the end of a lead. She saw teenagers kissing; I saw a blighted pregnancy and years of misery. She saw an elderly couple with the weekly shopping; I saw a pair of cadavers, tied together by nothing but groceries.

I once found her diary and read it. She kept mentioning someone called "Grump". It took me a while to get the reference.

"What are you doing in there?" asks MacMurrough.

I sit on the edge of the bed and calculate. It is only seven weeks since we lay upon this mattress together.

Sept semaines.

Quarante-neuf jours.

I turn face down, like a bather resting on a lilo, and I inhale the perfume and sweat of strangers. I dive down to a reef of lost aromas, a subterranean pool filled with transients darting in and

47

out through the waving kelp of time. I paddle with my fingertips and tread with my feet. I search for her, but she is gone.

To fucking France.

Outside, in the hallway, MacMurrough talks on the phone. I can't make out the words, but I can hear the occasional whistling syllable. He's from the *wesht* of Ireland where a *shtick* isn't a comedy routine, but a weapon for beating your cows. He hangs up and runs up the stairs.

Six months ago, I fixed a headboard onto the bed. She painted a watercolour of a ballerina and pinned it to the wall. We bought eggs and made omelettes. We smoked hash oil and drank Cinzano. She read *The Hobbit* and other weird stuff about big-eared pixies. I read *Motorcycle News* and a book about Aleister Crowley, the bow-tied Cambridge bisexual and *doppelganger* of Curly, from the Three Stooges.

I dive deeper. The light disappears. The shipping lanes fade into a hum as I close my eyes and sleep with the fishes. Bathed by the warmth of the Gulf Stream and rocked by the North Atlantic Drift, my snores insert themselves into bubbles and glide upwards.

There is a slapping on the door. I pull myself from the depths. It repeats. I light a cigarette. It repeats.

In 1161, Dermot MacMurrough's historic namesake blinded, kidnapped and castrated anyone who upset him. He smashed down the doors of monasteries and convents; he raped the Abbess of Kildare. His Irish kingdom seized, he went overseas looking for assistance. But where would a sociopathic rapist kidnapper go?

Fucking France.

Where else?

The slapping grows louder. It's time for me to step outside, unlock MacMurrough's bicycle, and beat him around the house with it. I am just about to pull the bolt when a voice from the other side barks, "Open up. Police."

This interesting turn of events prompts an immediate inventory: half an ounce of hash in back pocket; four grams of amphetamine sulphate, inside breast. A grand total of six months in Wormwood Scrubbs.

"Open up! Police!"

I put on my best Paddy-from-the-silage-pit accent.

"Wha' do ya' want?"

"I want you to open this door. You are trespassing."

"Forgive those who trespass against us."

"That'll be up to the magistrate."

"Wha's your name?"

"PC Dylan."

"Any relation of Bob?"

"Just open the fucking door."

Speaking of Bob Dylan ... When I was fifteen years old, I pitched a tent on a bluff overlooking the Irish Sea. A campfire threw bright orange sparks into the night sky. A bunch of Dublin kids stopped and asked for a cigarette, which I didn't give them. They were rough and ready and full of high jinks, and it was hard to tell if they were on a weekend break or if they had run away from home. Dubliners always look like they're in the wrong place, when they're not in Dublin.

They wobbled off along the beach, shouting and pushing each other into the lapping water. The girls carried their shoes in their hands. The boys took the shoes and threatened to throw them in the water, but didn't. They were wild, it appeared, but not unkind.

A while later, two girls in denim jeans and T-shirts came up and admired the fire. One of them looked like Faye Dunaway and the other was the spitting image of Bob Dylan, which is not a good look in a woman. They were both very high.

"Can we share your fire?" they asked, even though the night wasn't cold. They sat across from me, beaming through the smoke. They said their fathers were doctors and they were staying in a caravan at Tara Cove, and it was so boring, trying to get Radio Luxembourg on the wireless, watching couples sponging their babies in blue plastic tubs. They had to get out.

"We have microdots and morning glory seeds. Heavenly Blues."

I wasn't interested in the morning glory seeds because I'd heard they made you sick, but I took the LSD.

We walked down the beach collecting driftwood. Bob found a starfish and wondered if it would burn. "It is dead, isn't it?" she asked, and then, scared and uncertain, she flung it into the moving tide.

We got back to the tent and fed the fire, and somebody, I think it was Faye Dunaway, said of the flames, "It looks just like the sun."

"Same principle," I said.

They found this hilarious. They kept repeating it in different tones until it became truly absurd.

"Walking is like running," said Bob.

"Same principle," replied Faye.

They exploded in laughter.

"You look like a prophet," said Bob. "Do you have any words of wisdom?"

"Yes," I replied. "Never take a job in a tampon factory – there's bound to be strings attached."

They laughed and blushed. We mugged and smirked, but then the fire faded and we all looked desolate. When they stood to leave, Bob stared at me and I stared at Faye. She turned away.

Fifteen years old, she was more comfortable with her mind than she was with her body.

They walked off, leaving me with embers and a ghost ship parallel to shore, a distant speck of port-hole light pinned to the horizon. Everything was spinning; even the pitch-black darkness revolved like an empty wheel. I didn't feel great. I crawled into the tent. Everyone is cured, once they lie down. Except for Jimi Hendrix.

Later, the zip on the tent opened, and a silhouette slipped in beside me.

"It's me," she said. "I knew you wanted me to come back."

Was it Bob or Faye? I couldn't be sure.

She got undressed and squeezed into the sleeping bag.

I felt her face, like a blind man, her nose, her mouth. I was like a child squeezing plasticine.

"Why are you touching me like that?" she asked.

I couldn't tell her the truth.

"Do you want me to light a match?" she asked.

"No."

I touched her ears and her neck. She was a jumble of womanhood. She was every woman on the planet, but was she the one I wanted?

The great thing about acid is the power it has to bring about transubstantiation. Walls become portals. Fire turns into water. Flesh and blood can take on any shape you want. I blinked and the tent lit up like a prison break. Everything was visible as the searchlight flashed in a slow circle: my red-frame rucksack and the bright aluminium tent poles. Her jeans, T-shirt, and bra pushed into the angle between canvas and groundsheet. I pulled back her hair and pinned it behind her ears. It was like watching a picture develop in a darkroom. Lines and shadows joined.

Undefined arcs turned into eyebrows. A philtrum solidified and bridged the space between nose and mouth. The image assembled, all high cheekbones and pouting lips. Faye Dunaway, just as she looked in *Bonnie and Clyde* – minus the bullet holes. I was relieved. I could never put a length into Mr Zimmerman.

"I haven't done this before," she said.

"It's just like riding a bike," I replied.

"Same principle," she giggled.

When I awoke in the morning, she was gone. I wasn't sure what had happened, or with whom it had happened, or if it had happened at all, but then I got out of the sleeping bag and noticed a smudge of blood from my bare thigh to my navel. Naked, I took a walk down the beach as far as the shipwreck where barnacles ate rust and the whelk and gulls ate the barnacles. I felt free as I walked into the cold Irish Sea, and when the water came up to my waist, I washed her away, whoever she was.

"Open the door," says PC Dylan.

"You could be anyone," I reply. "By Jayzus, you mightn't even be a copper!"

"Open the door and you'll find out soon enough."

"I wasn't born yesterday," I say. "Come round to the window and gimme a look at you."

"I'm telling you to open this door!"

"And I'm telling you to come round to the window."

The hall door opens. I step into the shadows and wait. PC Dylan appears beyond the net curtain. He cups his hands to the glass and tries to see inside. The pride of Hendon Police College, he's young and gormless and his nose leaves a wet smudge on the pane. He looks like a beagle trapped in an aquarium. He turns away, angrily, and storms back around the house.

It's time for a discreet exit. I pop out of the room and pull the door behind me, then bound up the steps to the bathroom, where I find a damp plaid shirt on a hanger. Downstairs, PC Dylan shouts at the door.

"All right, that's it. Out you come!"

He looks upwards as I come sauntering down, carrying the shirt.

"Oi," I say in my best cor-blimey-guvnor South London accent, "what's going on here, mate?"

"Who are you?"

I tell him I'm Nobby Shoults, that's S-H-O-U-L-T-S, not Schultz, originally from Dagenham, but now resident in flat number five. I'm on my way to the clothes line because the baby threw up on my clobber. PC Dylan looks at me with wide, stupefied eyes. He wasn't expecting this much information. He turns back and pounds on the door.

"Oi! Don't you be playing silly buggers with me!"

"Is he playing silly buggers?" I ask.

"He's taking the piss, this one. Had me on a wild goose chase around the house."

I lower my voice. "He's trouble, that Paddy, him and his mate upstairs."

PC Dylan is instantly interested. "He has a mate upstairs?"

"Another Irish bloke. Flat eight. Dermot MacMurrough. Shifty geezer. The pair of 'em is always coming and going in the middle of the night with packages and such. You often hear them singing Irish songs. Sometimes you hear them going at it." To emphasise the point, I ram an index finger into a fist and slide it in and out. PC Dylan is shocked. Can it be that he has actually stumbled across a nest of Homo-Provos?

I excuse myself, but PC Dylan is lost in dreams of future glory. He unsnaps the handset from his Motorola radio and fills the hall with static. As I walk towards the exit, I see a small note pinned to the wallpaper beside the letterbox:

> PLEASE FORWARD MY POST TO:
> *447, Rue Jacob*
> *Paris 75006*
> *France*

It is signed *Kim Sutton*. I pull it from the wall and tuck it into my pocket. Outside, I toss the shirt into a box hedge and stride towards the tube station.

8

THIGH

In the summer of 1978, not long before we left for London, Kim Sutton took a job as a nurse's aide in a psychogeriatric ward. They told her she would have to feed, dress, bathe and groom the patients. I told her I'd join the army and kill people before I'd pick up a sponge and wash them.

On her first day, an old woman bit the tip off one of her own fingers because she thought her hands were covered in snakes. She ran down a corridor squirting blood and laughing, and when the nurses caught her, they tied her wrists to a bed with gauze bandages. "They showed me how to do a clove hitch," said Kim Sutton.

After about a week, she was transferred to the men's ward. She said the men were far more civilised than the women. They referred to her as "Miss". Some of them called her "little girl". The old men watched news on the television but they got spooked whenever Margaret Thatcher came on. "I think it's the voice," said Kim Sutton. "Because they don't look away, but they always cover their ears."

I asked her if she could get any pills but she pretended not to hear me. I could only imagine the sort of medication given to people who laughed as they chewed off their fingers.

This was Kim Sutton's first job, apart from some babysitting. When she was babysitting there'd been an episode where a man exposed himself.

"His wife went upstairs and he called me into the lounge. He was just sitting there... with it out."

The way she described it, she might have been talking about a pet hamster released from its cage.

"What did you do?" I asked.

"The babysitting money was on the coffee table, so I picked it up and counted it."

"You counted it?"

"Of course," she said. "I always counted the money."

To her it made perfect sense. If a man was prepared to whip out his cock in front of a fifteen-year-old, he was probably capable of financial impropriety.

"Did he say anything?"

"No. What could he say?"

She had the composure of a war correspondent reporting on the latest atrocity, a witness to something inevitable and pointless. She counted seven pounds in notes and change as her employer gradually went flaccid.

"You could have reported him. To someone."

She looked at me with incredulity. "It was a nice house," she said. "I liked going there."

Kim Sutton had grown up in a house filled with clamour. A dozen kids and the chaos they brought. When she came up to my home with the heavy red drapes, the thick walls, and the hardwood doors, she would revel in the tranquility of it. "I love it here," she'd say. "It's so peaceful and quiet ... and nobody's coming home pregnant."

"He exposed himself!" I said. "And you're acting as if it was no big thing."

She made a teensy gesture with her fingers and said, "It wasn't."

She was impossible to understand. Whenever I looked into her eyes and asked, "What's going on in there?" she always hit me with the same reply: "You'll never know."

After the babysitting incident, I wasn't exactly over the moon about her working in a men's ward, but she told me she wasn't alone. There was another girl, Isadora, who had cropped blonde hair and bright green eyes. "She's cute," said Kim Sutton.

"If Isadora is up for it," I said. "Maybe the three of us could do stuff together?"

She knew what I meant, but she said, "Like what? Go cycling?"

Over the next several weeks she told me about life on the ward. Mr French had been a tailor; he'd once made a suit for Éamon De Valera. Mr Wall was a chain smoker, addicted to Woodbines. Mr Hannigan and Mr Currie played cards all day, and Mr Cohen had once owned a furniture shop on the South Circular Road. I wasn't much interested in the old boys, but I was curious about Isadora. I pumped Kim Sutton for information. She revealed the small confidences she would have kept to herself, had I not been so insistent. She told me that Isadora was an only child, her parents separated. She lived on chocolate biscuits and milky tea. Her boyfriend was a quiet farm boy, and she was scared he would dump her because she talked too much.

One evening, I met Kim Sutton after work. She was upset. She said, "Mr Lovett is dead."

"Which one was he?"

"He played the accordion," she said.

I told her the accordion wasn't an instrument, it was just a big box of shame with straps on it. This seemed to upset her and I had to coax out the rest of the story.

She had been feeding one of the other old men with a spoon when she noticed that Mr Lovett was looking pale. She asked him if he was all right, but he couldn't reply. He just kept staring at her with an indescribable ferocity.

"His eyes ran all over me," she said.

"All over you?"

She told me that his lips trembled and he swallowed air in short little gulps. This raised my suspicions. "Tell me this," I said. "Were his hands outside the blankets or under the blankets?"

"You're disgusting," she said.

She didn't understand. The brightness of her beauty was no match for the darkness in a man's heart. She asked Mr Lowett if he was okay and he just stared at her, his mouth hanging open.

"Then his breathing stopped and I thought he was gone, but he wasn't. His eyes were still alive and they covered me, from top to toe. When his eyes stopped moving, I went and fetched the nurse."

He was old and dead and I was still jealous because he had captured Kim Sutton. He had dragged her away into the underworld, like a pervert taking a child into the bushes. I knew what I would have done, had I been there. I would have stepped between them and blocked his view. I would have broken the magic cord that tied his dirty old brain to a fit young body. I would have deprived him. I would have put a hand over his eyes, maybe his mouth too, and wherever he was going, he could have gone there alone. I didn't tell her any of this. I just said, "Well, that's one less accordion in the world."

Then it happened again. Old Mr Hannigan took a seizure and grabbed her thigh.

"Your thigh?"

She indicated a spot six inches north of her kneecap.

"Did you try and remove it? His hand?" I asked.

"It was a death grip," she said.

"Yeah, right. On your thigh."

"He had some sort of heart condition. It gave him involuntary twitches and then he had to grab stuff."

"Yeah. Your thigh."

"I think you're missing the point," she said. "He's the second man to die on my ward in ten days."

I knew she wanted me to tell her that it wasn't her fault, but I wasn't so sure. She gave these old guys a jolt. A shot of nervous electricity ran through them whenever she was around. If they had been watched over by a frumpy matron in support stockings, they might have lasted another ten years.

I finally got to meet Isadora. One night the three of us met up in a restaurant on Suffolk Street. I discovered pretty quickly that *cycling* would not be on the menu. Isadora despised me. The only thing we had in common was our shared desire to own Kim Sutton.

I made a joke about the old men popping their clogs, and Isadora reached across the table to pat Kim Sutton's hand. "They meant a lot to you, Mr Lovett and Mr Hannigan, didn't they?" Then she turned to me and said, "You shouldn't make jokes about them."

I pulled out a pen and handed it to her. "Here," I said. "Why don't you make a list of all the things I'm not allowed say in front of my girlfriend?"

Kim Sutton tried to steer the conversation towards safer ground. She said, "Isadora's boyfriend has a motorcycle, too."

He had a 350, I had a 250. It didn't matter that my Italian

beauty could piss his Jap crap off the road. It was a question of size. It's always about size. Women pretend they're above it all, but still they pity the flat-chested girl.

I went downstairs to the gents and when I returned, I caught a glimpse of Isadora giving Kim Sutton's thigh a sympathetic squeeze, just like the old dead guy, and it pressed a button inside me. I sat back down and gave Isadora a cold stare. She took out a tube of chapstick and lubed up her lips. She knew it was on. She started talking about work, a sure way to exclude me. She prattled on about "poor old Mr Currie" who had no one to play cards with now that "dear old Mr Hannigan" was gone. She told a long and winding anecdote about Mr Cohen's threadbare slippers and the fact that he often wore them on the wrong feet. Sometimes the ward was too cold and sometimes too hot; they never got the temperature right. Why did visitors always bring newspapers, and why was it always the *Evening Herald*? The old men didn't read. Had they forgotten or had they lost interest? What sort of party would they have for Christmas? The old boys liked pulling the Christmas crackers, but their disappointment could be unbearable if the explosions weren't big enough. I pictured cardboard tubes, covered with glitter and stuffed with TNT. Severed hands and arms flying around the ward. Isadora droned on about soft food and the games you could play with alphabet soup.

She paused and refreshed her lips with chapstick. I reached down and put my hand on Kim Sutton's thigh. Isadora noticed and her eyes opened wide.

On she went about mashed potatoes and music from the 1940s, confusing Glenn Miller with Glen Campbell, and thereby providing me with an interesting image of the Rhinestone Cowboy drowning in the English Channel. All the time she spoke, her eyes were fixed on my hand. I squeezed and massaged. Kim Sutton twisted, but she couldn't get away. The restaurant turned into a giant magnifying glass, with a hand and a thigh at the centre of focus.

Isadora's speed of delivery slowed. My hand moved up another inch, above the agreed line of human decency. The words continued to flow, but the point and direction became even more uncertain. It was like watching a ship in full sail being confronted by a pirate with one deadly remaining cannonball.

"Your boyfriend is right," I said. "You do talk too much." Boom! Right below the waterline. The ship stopped on a dime. Isadora looked at Kim Sutton in panic. It was obvious that her "best friend" had let her down. What other little secrets had she shared with me between the pillow and the pulled-up blanket?

Isadora looked at her watch and said, "I really have to go." She waved away Kim Sutton's protests. "No, no. I have to go. I have to now. Please." She knocked over a chair in her haste to escape. She ran past the restaurant window, down Suffolk Street, towards the bus stop outside Trinity College.

It was a while before Kim Sutton spoke. "Why did you do that?" she asked.

"Why?" It was hard to believe that she didn't get it. Why didn't matter. Why never matters. Questions that start with "why" don't deserve an answer. I finally let go of her thigh. Why?

"I won," I said. "Didn't I?"

9

CONVENT

I got all my girlfriends, including Kim Sutton, from the same source: Saint Bridget's Convent on the Dublin Road. Their school uniform was a myrtle green jacket and skirt, white shirt, knee socks and black patent leather shoes. There was another girls' school in town, The Presentation Academy for Young Ladies. I didn't care much for their navy pinafore and gingham accoutrements; it looked like the sort of costume an escaped mad woman would steal from a clothes-line.

My earliest girlfriends were mostly pale creatures, their faces easily lost in a crowd. But there was one exception, a girl with a name so preposterously Irish, she could only have been American. Colleen McIlvaney of Brooklyn, New York. She was a gum-chewer and a nose-talker, but there was something sexy about her crooked smile and her habit of pushing boys around with her breasts. Colleen's father had sent her to St. Bridget's as a full-time boarder. He wanted her to experience a complete Catholic education at the hands of women who knelt to pray, sat to teach and stood to pee. She hated every minute of it.

I met her at a "social" organised by the nuns and the Christian

Brothers. Boys and girls were brought together for polite conversation broken by musical interludes. Sometimes a boy would play a tin whistle and a girl would dance in the old style. With arms limp by her side and legs as straight as stair rods, she would murder passion with every jump and jiggedy-boo. It was like watching a reanimated corpse battling *rigor mortis*.

During our social chat, nuns and Brothers sat around the outer perimeter of the assembly hall, sipping tea and watching. I told Colleen that I was studying higher level geography, history, biology and English. I told her that I played basketball and that I had been on the school debating team two years in a row. I told her that I was a decent swimmer and enjoyed listening to LPs on my record player. When it was her turn to talk, she leaned in close and said, "I want you to pinch my nipples."

My eyes widened.

"You heard me," she said. "I want you to twist 'em like you're tuning a radio with one hand and opening a safe with the other."

I laughed. The nuns and the Brothers bristled. Antennae and periscopes rose from their ranks.

Colleen whispered, "I wanna meet you on Friday night, beside the tennis courts."

"What time?"

"Nine o'clock."

I met her twice a week for the next seven weeks. She crept down the fire-escape and I climbed the convent wall. We took walks around the hockey field, stepping into the bushes every few yards, kissing and fumbling. She lifted her skirt and took my hand. The nuns in their nearby beds felt the electricity generated by our actions. Their thighs tingled and they bit their sleeping tongues when Colleen McIlvaney came.

It took me a while to realise that Colleen was actually trying to get kicked out of school and bounced all the way back home to Brooklyn. She started asking questions like, "Did anybody see you getting over the wall?" and when I said no, she was clearly disappointed. What she really needed was a one-man band tossing flashbangs and singing "Wake Up Little Sister" as he marched across the tennis court in jackboots. I was too discreet.

My final failure as a boyfriend came just before Christmas. Colleen gave me a fancy cigarette lighter, a Ronson Varaflame, with my name engraved on top. I gave her a bottle of perfume ("Kinda new. Kinda wow – Charlie!"). It cost two quid. She called me cheap, which in Ireland is considered a compliment. In fact I was thoughtless and inconsiderate. If she had stuck around a bit longer, she might have discovered the difference.

After four months in the psychogeriatric ward, Kim Sutton had reached the end of the line. "Another old man died today," she said.

"Jesus," I said. "You stop hearts the way some nurses stop erections."

She wasn't amused. She told me she was moving to the city to look for work. That knocked me back. I told her that the city was a hostile place, full of drippy-nosed hooligans in anoraks, purse-snatchers and Peeping Toms. "And you don't have anywhere to stay," I said.

Knowing full well that she was aiming a spear straight at my heart, Kim replied, "I'll be staying with Colleen McIlvaney."

"You mean Colleen tennis court, Ronson Varaflame, orgasm in the bushes McIlvaney?"

"Yes, that one."

I was beyond stunned. Girlfriends don't move in with ex-girlfriends, except in blue movies. For a moment I pictured them showering together. "You gotta sponge me good," said Colleen, in my fevered dream.

Kim Sutton judged my expression and asked, "Are you thinking what I think you're thinking?"

"Does it involve soap?" I asked. "If so, yes."

I told her it was a bad idea. How well did they know each other?

"We sat in the same classroom for five years," she said.

Right. I'd forgotten about that.

Colleen had found an apartment on Rathgar Avenue, in a building with a buzzer on the front door and ficus and philodendron trees in the lobby. The way Kim Sutton described it, it was urban, sophisticated and smug, like something out of the Mary Tyler Moore show.

With Kim Sutton gone, it rained more than ever in the Rainy Town. I walked down by the river and shouted abuse at the swans. I got stoned every night with people I hated. I looked for hell and I found it.

She came back home at the weekends and told me Capital City stories about fifty-pound scarves in the window of Brown Thomas. She told me about the Dandelion Market and the gigs in the National Stadium.

"Colleen says hello," she said.

"Tell Colleen hello back," I said, in a voice that was airy and mean.

Colleen worked in the new burger joint on Grafton Street. They hired her because she "sounded New York." She wore a rust-coloured uniform with a big yellow logo. She gave away free burgers to everyone she knew, and if you handed her a five-pound note, she gave you ten back in change.

My hopes of Kim Sutton returning home in failure were dashed when she found a job in a French restaurant on Wicklow Street. Le Petit Chou. It was owned by a pair of brothers, Iggy and Sam, and the kitchen was run by a French chef called Maximilian. Their names alone were enough to guarantee my undying hatred. I pictured them posing with skillets and strings of garlic around their necks, a suckling pig turning on a spit in the background. I had never been in a fancy restaurant, so my imaginings tended towards the medieval.

"What sort of people eat there?" I asked.

"Politicians from Leinster House," she said. "German tourists. We get a lot of food critics."

That was so fucking Irish, a restaurant kept afloat by the people sent to sink it. I went back to the river and ordered the swans out of town. "If you're not gone by Tuesday," I roared, "I'll be back with a shotgun and a hungry Cocker Spaniel!"

Weeks passed and the friendship between Colleen and Kim Sutton deepened. They confided in one another. They shared dreams and expectations.

"Does Colleen ever mention me?" I asked.

"No."

"Never?"

"She just laughs whenever I say your name."

So I was a source of amusement. A romantic novelty. An amorous automaton. A wind-up cock. I put on my poker face and pretended it didn't matter. But young men were creeping into their lives. They were referred to as "friends" who came around to "move furniture" and "paint spare rooms," but male "friends" only do that stuff if they're looking for sex. A man would carry a grand piano up four flights of stairs if he thought there was a handjob at the end of it.

Kim Sutton told me she spoke French at work. Everybody did. Le Petit Chou was a Parisian oasis. "It's fully immersive," she said. "We feel completely French."

"Really?" I said. "Do you ever feel like surrendering to the German tourists?"

She was slipping into a new world, a world in which my central position was no longer guaranteed. A world full of unpainted rooms and moveable furniture, French conversation and shop windows filled with delights.

There is only one thing Earth can do if the moon starts to drift beyond its field of gravity. Earth has no choice. Earth must move to Dublin.

I found a bedsit in Ballsbridge. Never mind swinging a cat, it wasn't big enough for a cat to swing a mouse. The bed was no wider than a stretcher and the "kitchenette" was a wonky hot-plate in a closet. My housemates were mostly Spanish and Italian students who spent all their time in the shared bathroom.

I found a job as a kitchen porter in Dublin's finest hotel, hauling buckets of soup from the stockpots, scrubbing salamanders and mopping floors with buckets of steaming water and sugar soap. I had two work companions, a pair of skinny Dubliners called Bob and Shay. They stole Pernod and brandy from the sauces corner. They stole meat from the fridges. They walked about with roast chickens hidden beneath their greasy shop coats. They were magicians. Everything around them disappeared.

I lasted three weeks in Dublin's finest hotel, but they fired me when they discovered I had no soul. I got a new job as a stagehand in Dublin's grandest theatre, pulling levers and throwing switches for a fucking tedious Mime & Mask troupe from Switzerland. They moved on the darkened stage in black velvet body-suits. They reminded me of cats; I wanted to put them all in plastic bags and toss them into the Grand Canal. "Mime your way out of that," I would say.

The Swiss cast was troubled by my murderous stares and

sneering demeanour. Plus I was stoned all the time. At the end of week one, the curtain came down on my theatrical career.

I moved back to the Rainy Town. The swans were gone and there was no one left to shout at. I never told Kim Sutton about my Dublin sojourn. I had moved around that city like one of the Swiss mimes, creating no impact and leaving no impression. On a Friday evening I would catch the early train down the country, and she would arrive back an hour later. I'd wait in the station to meet her. "How was your week?" she would ask.

"Same as yours," I'd reply, and it was almost the literal truth.

There were nights in Dublin when I lurked in the shadows and followed her home at a distance. She hopped on a bus and I took a taxi. She stopped at the late night shop in Rathmines to buy an orange and a women's magazine; I stood in a doorway and smoked a joint. She walked across Leicester Avenue and Kenilworth Square with the sort of confidence a young girl doesn't usually have after dark; I crept behind her like an alien creature dodging the peasants with pitchforks. One night I watched the lights go on and off in her apartment as she moved from room to room. Another night, I climbed into the box hedge at the front of the building. I saw Colleen McIlvaney arrive home, ironically striding up the street like the model in the Charlie perfume ad. She looked prettier than I remembered, but she was less desirable now that she was free and at large in the world. I had wanted her most when she was locked away in a convent, in the chamber of sanctified virginity.

"Hello?" said Colleen, scanning the box hedge. "Anybody there?"

She couldn't have seen me, but somehow her senses prickled. It was just like old times at the edge of the tennis court, except this time I wouldn't step out and reveal my wicked intentions.

Back in the Rainy Town, I waited for news from the front.

Eventually it came, and it was good. Colleen had been fired from her job in the burger joint. A drunk had tumbled up to the counter one night. "Why don't you let me grab those tits?" he'd asked.

"Why don't you let me stick this cheeseburger up yer fuckin' ass?" she'd replied.

The management had not been happy. A man in a white shirt had shaken his head and pointed at the door. Colleen, it appeared, was too New York for Grafton Street. A week later she was back in Brooklyn and Kim Sutton was distraught. Colleen's father had been paying for the apartment. Reality was scratching at the door. "What will I do?" Kim Sutton asked. "I love living in the city."

Fortunately I had a plan. I had managed to save three hundred pounds and I had asked my friend Kevin if we could come and stay with him in London.

"London," said Kim Sutton. "I don't know."

I told her London would be just like Dublin, only bigger and brighter and packed with more possibilities. "It's London or the Rainy Town," I said.

A cloud passed over her face, but I knew it would clear and sense would prevail. Dublin had never connected with me. It had belonged to Kim Sutton. But London would be mine, all mine, and if she was lucky, I might just share it with her.

10

BOY

"A mother who loses her child can no longer believe in God."
Victor Hugo, *The Hunchback of Notre-Dame.*

SUNDAY, MAY 6, 1979

The boy had a mouth like a twisted rag. He stood in the doorway of the house at Tottenham Green and looked us up and down. We needed engine parts for a Honda 175.

"It's out back," he said. "I'm breaking it for scrap."

The boy led us through the house. His mother walked past carrying a ball of laundry. Her eyes were aimless. All she knew was that the world dumped pain and washing at her feet every day, and it didn't matter that her son was leading strangers through the messed-up living room.

The back yard was full of junk. Sheets of de-laminated plywood covered some of the wreckage, but most of it was out in the open: a blue bathroom suite; a wardrobe with a cracked mirror; a plastic fertiliser sack stuffed with shoes; a guitar with a missing neck; and two solid bags of old cement.

"Cool stuff," said Kevin.

The boy didn't get it. He puffed himself up with the pride of ownership. He pulled back a tattered Union Jack and revealed a smashed-up piano.

"Someday I'll restore that, and I'll play it."

Kevin gave him a look that said, *No, you won't. You will never fix anything because you belong to a breed that breaks, wrecks, smashes and ruins, and then you collect the debris. Your father, your grandfather and your great-grandfather were damagers and destroyers and they passed down their toxic DNA in a series of short bedroom grunts – to you. You, my child, are about as useful as a fucking pogo stick in a minefield.*

The boy grinned as he tinkled on a fractured key. There was a scampering animal sound inside the piano. The boy stepped back quickly and slammed down the lid.

"The Honda 175," said Kevin. "We need the piston rings."

The boy pulled aside the drum of an old tumble dryer and the wing of a car to reveal the barest skeleton of a motorcycle. The back wheel was missing, the petrol tank was missing, the indicator stems dangled from electrical threads, the handlebars were gone, and the speedometer glass was cracked. The engine was still in place only because the demon of carnage had run out of destructive energy.

"You'll need a 10-, a 12- and an 18-millimetre socket," said Kevin.

"I know what I need, mate," the boy sniffed. "I'll go get my tools."

"You do that, *mate*," said Kevin.

The boy went into the house and Kevin rolled a joint. "What do you think of Quasimodo?" he said. I was baffled. Kevin laughed. "You didn't notice the hunchback?"

I said no, I hadn't.

The door opened and the boy's mother came out with another giant ball of laundry. Kevin nodded at the rusty drum that lay in the middle of the yard. "Will we pop it in the tumble dryer?" he asked, holding out the joint in her direction. She was a drab, thirty-something woman in apron and slippers with a life that had stopped moving sometime in the 1960s. She took the joint and stuck it in the side of her mouth. The big ball of laundry dripped on her hip as she took two deep drags. She blew a lungful of smoke into the space between us, and then chased it with a cough. She handed back the joint and went about her business.

We watched her hang the laundry, then prop it up with a wooden pole. She went back inside and the boy came out. He carried a tin bucket filled with an assortment of greasy tools: sockets, screwdrivers, a cold steel chisel and a clawhammer. The boy put a ring spanner on the 12-millimetre bolt and it spun without catching.

"Imperial," said Kevin. "That's half inch. You need metric."

"I know what I need, mate," said the boy.

I couldn't take my eyes off the lump on his back. How had I missed it? It sat between his shoulders like the birth of another head.

The boy tried to clamp the nut with a vise-grips, but the tool was old and rusty and the jaws wouldn't lock. The boy reached into the bucket and pulled out the chisel and hammer. One by one, he sheared off the eight retaining nuts. Kevin winced every time. He wasn't great with people, but he would never hurt an engine.

The boy lifted up the metal cover and grinned. "All right mate?" he said, and then he poked into the opening with a flat screwdriver and pried off the clip on the cam chain. The chain itself dropped into the depths of the gearbox. Kevin closed his eyes and shook his head.

"See," the boy said, "*that's* how you do it."

The cylinder head did not separate immediately because the years had turned the gasket to glue. The boy smacked it with the hammer and a cluster of brittle cooling fins snapped off. He kicked them aside. He hit it again and the head tilted. Two more heavy blows and it fell to the ground, revealing the block and the pistons in their sleeves.

"There's the pistons!" said the boy with some excitement. He reached in and tried to pull the engine block free. It didn't budge. The boy kicked it with the heel of his shoe. Nothing happened. He tried to force the screwdriver between the block and the gearbox, but there wasn't a razor blade of space. He couldn't wedge, lever or force the obstinate lump.

"If I had penetrating oil," said the boy, "I'd have it out in a flash."

"But you don't have penetrating oil," said Kevin.

"No," the boy replied, "but I do have petrol."

Kevin looked at me and said, "He's got petrol."

The boy went to a shed half buried in trash. He pulled open the sheet of corrugated metal that acted as a door. He disappeared, and when he emerged, he was carrying a milk bottle filled with a yellowish liquid. He sloshed it into both cylinders. It spilled out over the gearbox and onto the ground where it formed a rainbow puddle.

"That's going to penetrate," the boy said, "and once that penetrates, the whole thing will slide away like butter. Like butter, mate. Wait and see."

I didn't know much about things mechanical, but I knew that petrol did not have the same properties as penetrating oil.

We waited.

After two or three minutes the boy said, "That should be

enough." He kicked the engine once more and the petrol sloshed out. The block was as tight as ever.

"Do you know what we need?" said the boy. "We need to force the pistons back down in the sleeves."

The boy went into the shed and returned with a pickaxe. Kevin's eyes widened.

The boy hefted the pickaxe over his shoulder. The handle rested on the ball of his hump.

"Heigh-ho, heigh-ho," said Kevin. "It's off to work we go."

The boy didn't get it. "One smack," he said, "slap bang in the middle of the crown, that's all it needs." He turned to Kevin, looking for agreement, but Kevin remained inscrutable.

The boy swung the pick-axe and the sharp point tore through the centre of the piston. It smashed the aluminium and plunged six or seven inches into the very guts of the engine.

"Good shot," said Kevin, lighting another joint.

"It was, wasn't it?" The boy replied, but the piston hadn't budged, not even a fraction. The boy took the end of the pick-axe handle and wiggled it. He rocked it, he shook it, he kicked it and he knelt upon it. "I'm going to take it out and try again," he said. He grabbed the head of the pick-axe and tried to withdraw it, but it had become part of the motorcycle.

"Excalibur," said Kevin, but the boy didn't get it.

The boy climbed onto the frame, put all his weight on the pick-axe handle, and started jumping up and down. The motorcycle promptly keeled over and the boy landed awkwardly. The last dregs of petrol flooded out on the ground and rolled towards the piano. The boy swore. He took the hammer and bashed the seat. He bashed the frame. He smashed the headlight. "You're a bastard," he said to the motorcycle. "A bastard."

There was blood on the boy's hand from the fall. A splinter of engine fin had lodged in his palm. He pulled it out and pretended to feel no pain.

"What we need to do," the boy announced "is heat the bastard."

He poured the last drop of petrol into both cylinders and then asked Kevin for his box of matches.

"Are you sure that's wise?"

"Just gimme the matches, mate."

Kevin tossed the yellow box at the boy. I had a bad feeling. The boy struck a match and flicked it at the motorcycle. The inferno was instant. Flames shot out of the cylinders and set the foam in the seat alight. The clutch cable turned into a fiery snake and the carburettor popped. The wiring loom started to melt and toxic floaters drifted through the air like miniature umbrellas. A molten drip landed on the rainbow puddle and a blue wave flashed across the yard and into the mound of rubbish. The dry tinder in the piano ignited and the creature living within scratched in panic, creating a noise not unlike improvisational jazz.

The boy was shocked. It was as if he had never imagined that petrol and fire could make such poor bedfellows. He grabbed the ragged Union Jack and started beating the flames, but the flag caught fire and he tossed it onto the pyre.

Kevin took a long drag on the joint and then, improbably, started singing *Jerusalem*: "Bring me my bow of burning gold, Bring me my arrows of desire; Bring me my spear! O, clouds unfold! Bring me my chariot of fire!"

The boy still didn't get it. I looked to the kitchen window where the boy's mother stood at the sink, watching the flickering blaze. She turned on a tap and filled a basin with no great haste. She looked like a woman whose life would only get better if her house burned to the ground.

II

MOTO

FRIDAY, MAY 18, 1979

We are at the bus stop on Lordship Lane, ready to board the 243, when three youths with angry dogs approach us. They bar our way and the leader, a red-haired boy known as Ginger, with mannish aspirations and a face slashed twice with a razor blade, leans into the doorway and says to the driver, "These lads will be catching the next bus."

"I've been looking for you," says Kevin. "You owe me money."

Ginger turns to his two pals, "This facking Paddy takes my motorbike and says he can fix it. I don't see him for a month, and now he's telling me that I owe him dosh."

The two companions laugh. Kevin looks at Ginger, wide-eyed and hurt. "Let me tell you about your bike."

"I'm all ears."

Kevin explains how one of the valves came unseated and punched a hole in the piston and how this in turn blew the big-end bearings out of their shells. Ginger's face begins to sag under the weight of information and his two drones turn their scant attention towards the dogs.

"The bloke what gave me that bike says there was almost nothing wrong with it." Ginger sniffs.

"*Caveat emptor.*"

"Wot?"

"It's Gaelic for 'he saw you coming,'" says Kevin. "And I spent a full Saturday morning working on it. That's why you owe me money."

"I'm not giving you any facking money."

"Fine," says Kevin, addressing the full length and breadth of Lordship Lane. "Then you and your mates can hop on the next bus, come to my place and pick up your junk. It's a *back* yard I have, not a scrap yard."

Kevin stands akimbo and waits for a reaction. His whole demeanour is so forceful, earnest and convincing that I almost believe the bike is a rusting eyesore, a blot on the Tottenham landscape. I almost forget that ten days earlier we'd changed the piston rings, shortly before Kevin put an ad in the *Evening News*:

Honda 175 for sale. Perfect nick. £80.

I'd been there, too, when two fat brothers came to the house, handed over £75 and wobbled away without helmets.

"Come on," Kevin says, "You can drag that piece of shite back to where you found it."

"What am I supposed to do with a clapped-out bike?"

"Not my problem," Kevin says. "But if you prefer I can always leave it out for the council or the coppers."

"Let's not talk silly bollocks."

"Forty quid," Kevin says, and Ginger's eyeballs pop. The

henchmen gasp and even the dogs seems to slobber the words in disbelief.

Ginger's blood rises like a spring tide in a blowhole. His face turns pink and his fingers curl into small but dangerous fists.

"Twenty quid for repairing the bike," Kevin persists, "and another twenty quid for getting rid of it."

Not only is he demanding a ransom, he has already sold the hostage. This is the Kevin that never fails to amaze me.

We'd started our lives together, at the foot of the Blackstairs Mountains, playing games in haystacks and riding bicycles on hot summer tar. We looked at girls and they looked back. We stole a box of menthol cigarettes from the railway depot and gave them to the old men in the psychiatric hospital, thereafter referred to as "menthol patients".

After primary school, we travelled in different directions. I enrolled in the Academy to learn dead and crippled languages; Kevin went to the Tech, where they welded steel ribbons into the shape of infinity. But we both loved motorcycles and that tied us together. We rode down to Carnsore Point and Courtown, on back roads without road tax or insurance. We shouted at each other through raging wind: "Do you want to turn back?"

"No. Let's keep going."

One day we met on the bridge in the Rainy Town, and watched weeds flapping in the river current. Somebody played Jean Genie on a portable radio and Kevin said he was going to London. I didn't pay much attention because I thought it was an aspirational thing. He was only fifteen years old. A week later, he was gone.

Over the next three years, rumours and confusions filtered home. Kevin had found a job in a biscuit factory. He'd stolen a BMW and driven from London to Bristol with a girl he had charmed into riding behind him. He'd thrown a courtroom bible at a judge and got six months in Feltham Young Offenders'. He'd worked with a concrete crew on the building of the NatWest Tower. He was into jazz. He drove a Jensen Interceptor. He bought and sold amphetamine sulphate.

It was all true. Except the stuff about jazz.

Ginger turns to his mates. "Can you facking believe this Paddy?"

The mates shake their heads and a bus rumbles into view. Kevin betrays no emotion. The word "Paddy" never slaps him in the face; he just lets it roll right over him and disappear into 800 years of history. Ginger's hand slips inside his jacket pocket and I get the feeling that the day is on its way to a messy conclusion with blades, blood, witnesses, cops, ambulances, stretchers, transfusions, injections, last rites, next-of-kin, tears, beers and tombstones.

Ginger's hand emerges from his pocket, holding not a knife, but a note, a twenty-pound note showing William Shakespeare queenishly poncing against a stack of books. "Park that bike at the bottom of the canal," Ginger says as he snuffles a sagging drip back up into his nose, "and let's not talk about it again."

"I want forty," Kevin insists.

Ginger shakes his head. "You're a cheeky facking Paddy," he says, but he hands over another twenty-pound note.

The bus stops and the doors open, Ginger waves us aboard like an old-time concierge. "You take care of that business straight away," he says, "or there will be retro-cushions."

We climb upstairs and find seats at the front. The bus pulls away from the kerb and begins crawling through a valley of red-and brown-brick houses. We pull alongside Ginger and his mates. Kevin looks down at the pathetic expedition party of Union Jack parka jackets, Doc Martens and slobbering dogs. He is Amundsen observing Scott, triumphant but saddened. He hands me one of the twenty-pound notes as the bus picks up speed.

"That," he says, "is how they lost the Empire."

12

CON

I emerge from Piccadilly station and head for Wardour Street. Like my forebears, I am magnetically drawn to Soho. I like the steam that rises off the place and the dynamo that spins within. Besides, it's too early in the day to hit Ward's Irish House and watch the cavemen blowing their noses on the walls.

I turn onto Berwick Street and come across a small huddle of men standing around an upturned orange crate. Three heavily creased playing cards rest on the Jaffa label.

"Find the lady, find the lady, find the lady."

It's a small riot of noise and hubbub, a splash of chaos and row-tow-row.

"Come on, boys and girls, find the lady! Find the queen of hearts!"

With my fresh young face, I must look quite the mark. In fact I've heard about this scam, though I've never caught it in action.

A man in a suit, the so-called "toff", says: "Here, young lad, put your hand on this card and don't let anybody move it, 'specially not him [gesturing towards the "dealer"]. Don't let that bloke move it. He's trying to move it. He's trying to cheat me. He's trying to cheat me out of twenty quid. Keep your hand on that card. That's the red lady. Keep your hand on her while I get out my wallet."

I put my hand on the card.

"Good lad," the toff says as he pats his pockets in a grand gesture. "Now where did I put my lolly?"

To see into a man's soul, the best avenue is through the eyes, but the Victorians were right – to know a man's place in the world, look at his shoes. Worn-out leather and stitching that's ready to burst. Heels fading into tapered wedges. This toff is no toff.

The dealer has an anorak with a broken zip. His eyes are puffy from a high-salt diet, and oily strings of hair are hooked around his ears. He looks frantic, wounded and damp.

The man on my left and the man on my right are "spectators". They make a lot of noise, but their movements are tired and slow, as if they have done this routine so often they just can't be bothered anymore.

"Keep your finger on the card, mate," they both say, slowly and in unison.

Another accomplice stands on the corner of Peter Street. This is the "lookout". He's tall and nervous, with his fingers close to his mouth in case he needs to whistle.

"Let me get my money out, mate. Don't budge. This is a dead cert, son, a dead cert."

I wonder if they even know how to perform the sleight. Instead of showing me the lady, and then hiding her, they have dispensed with all finesse. I am to be swayed solely by the impeccable honesty of this tatty toff with his worn-out shoes and dilapidated suit. I feel cheated – not because I'm being cheated, but because they're giving me the abbreviated version of the con.

The toff says, "Here's my twenty quid," and wedges the note between my finger and the card. "You've done a great job. Tell you what, I'm going to let you in on it."

"No bloody way," the dealer says, faking comic-book shock.

"He's my mate. Helped me out, he did. I'm letting him in."

"That's only fair," the spectators say, slowly and in unison.

"What's your name, son?" asks the toff.

"Jude," I reply, for a lark. "I'm named after the saint."

Jude is the patron saint of lost causes, but they don't get the joke because they're stupid. And Protestant.

"Well, your mate Jude is looking out for you today," says the toff. "Now come on, before this bastard shuts up shop. Plant your twenty quid down on that card and we'll both be winners."

There is silence and calm all around me. These men have made their pitch. They have tried their pitiful best, and now their collective belly sucks itself in as they wait for a decision.

The whole thing is depressing beyond words. It's a sad wreck of a swindle. Twenty pounds divided by five men – what's the point? I could easily afford to let them have it. I make fifty pounds a day for dozing around in an office, and these blokes have given me nothing but fun in the five minutes I've known them. For pure entertainment value, it's almost a bargain, but I'm torn. Back in Ireland, a few short months ago, twenty pounds meant long hours stuck in the drawing office above the steelworks.

A memory takes me, and I'm back in the developing room, soaking up the stench from the ammonia box. I hear the low groan from the print machine and the near-constant sound of hammer on iron. I hear the punch of the drill presses, the buzz of the welders and the snap of the guillotine.

At five minutes to one, every day, two hundred men lump together in the yard, waiting for the big, blue gates to open. The timekeeper stands with his eyes fixed on the clock. Every day the same men, hidden in the dowdy safety of the crowd, call out the same things.

"C'mon for fuck's sake Freddy, open the gate. Open the gate and let us get the dinner. Come on, Freddy. Fuck you Freddy. Freddy you're a bastard. You are a cunt, Freddy."

The invective directed at Freddy hardens until the clock clicks "one" and the big bolt is drawn sideways.

"Good man Freddy. You're a star, Freddy. Fair fucks to you Freddy. Sound man, Freddy."

When the men are released, they're like racehorses with dementia. They run for twenty yards, and then forget the point.

One Christmas, the company gave a turkey to every worker. At finishing time, the men lurched along Barrack Street with their plucked bounty slung across their shoulders. They dragged their sacks of dead flesh into Flannagan's pub and tossed them into a pile in the corner. Pints of porter and chasers of Powers whiskey, cigarettes smoked and stubbed into the spaces between floorboards, hilarity and hi-jinks, complaints about managers coupled with fighting words: "He doesn't know who he's dealing with, but he'll know soon enough."

At closing time there were arguments concerning which turkey belonged to whom.

"Here, hang on a minute, mine had more bristles on the wing."

"Mine had pinker feet."

"Mine had a darker snood."

"Mine had a smile on his face!"

"Mine had the smell of strong drink on his breath."

Laughter de-fused the kerfuffle and they stumbled out into the frosty air, a mix of man and bird and rowdy spirits, their Christmas pay-packets looking the worse for wear.

The steelworks, the sugar factory or the dole office. That was your choice in the Rainy Town, and if you went for the latter you signed on twice a week in a circular queue designed by Dante. Three hundred souls exposed to the world, their small brown cards clutched in their hands, shoved deep in their pockets. If you asked the girls behind the counter about employment, they would hand you a photocopied leaflet about sheep-shearing opportunities in Australia.

Ireland has only two words for the job seeker: *G'day mate*!

I look at the hopeful, hopeless tricksters, and I know it wouldn't take much to make them happy. I could give them a hearty laugh and a cheery chuckle down the pub later on. But that's not going to happen.

"I don't have a twenty-pound note," I say, "but I do have a fifty."

The effect is immediate. It's as if somebody has taken these five men and hooked up their genitals to Battersea power station. Even the dealer, who is supposed to be convincing me otherwise, starts loosely nodding his head.

"You're a bloody dark horse, Jude," the toff says. "I bet you've played this game before."

"I don't know if I should risk it," I say, putting on my best bog-accent. "It's everything I brought over from Ireland. It's all I have. I mean to say... if I were to lose this..."

The toff slides in quickly. "Go on, mate, put your money down on the red lady. Double your fifty."

I ask myself why I dislike him so much. What is it about him?

I mean, beyond the sly familiarity, the nose that wrinkles, and the eyes that flutter? Is it that London way he pronounces the word "red", the pushing-out of the lower lip and the placing of a small "w" at the beginning : *wred*.

Put your money down on the wred lady.

My first day in this city I approached a taxi driver sitting in his cab outside Euston Station, reading the *Sun*. "Excuse me," I said. "Could you tell me which bus I take to Lordship Lane?"

The taxi driver had pushed out his lower lip, just like the toff, and said, "Get a red one, Paddy."

Get a wred one.

I could have bashed him there on the spot. I could have dragged him out the window of his Coventry crapmobile and sodomised him with his rolled up *Sun,* but I didn't. I turned and walked away.

"Are you sure?" I say to the toff. "Are you absolutely certain she's there?"

"On my grandmother's grave." He smiles the smile of a man who has just pushed his granny down the stairs.

"Tell you what," I say. "If I lose, the dealer can keep my fifty, but I'm keeping your twenty."

The toff looks at the dealer and the spectators look at each other. The silent click and rattle of mental maths. The toff wrinkles his nose and flutters his eyes. The spectators shift in unison. The lookout on the corner of Peter Street throws nervous glances in every direction. He's keen to whistle and be gone.

"All right," the toff says. "You and me are mates, Jude. Why not?"

"Show me your money," the dealer says.

I reach into my pocket, keeping one eye on the toff, one eye on the dealer and one finger on the twenty-pound note.

The sexual commerce of Soho pauses; all the hanky-panky and

the wanky-wanky. In the magazine exchanges on Walker's Court, the sticky pages stop flicking; the neon windmill is becalmed; and the girls in the changing rooms at Jo-Jo's stare at their perpetual pouts. The touts in their Harrington jackets holding out flyers that promise "Live Girls!" – always better than the other sort – transform into pot-bellied wax-works.

I love it when London stops.

My hand comes out of the pocket and with a shimmery clink, I drop a fifty-pence piece on the card.

Boom! The place explodes like Zabriskie Point. Everybody in the vicinity is injected with straight speed, including the fat man with the fruit stand who suddenly starts juggling oranges and avocados.

"What the fuck!" says the dealer.

"Are you kidding me, mate?" asks the toff. "*Fifty fucking pence?*"

The spectators turn to each other and mouth the same words: "Is he mucking about?"

The lookout on the corner of Peter Street can sense that something is wrong. His whistling fingers move towards his chin.

"Like I said, I don't have a twenty-pound note, but I do have a fifty."

"Do you think this is some sort of joke, Paddy?" says the toff.

"What happened to our friendship?" I reply. "A moment ago we were mates."

The toff reaches out to retrieve his money, but I shake my head and cover it with a hand. He knows he's not getting it back.

"A deal is a deal," I say.

"There's five of us," he says, but there is weakness in his voice. These men aren't fighters. They are whistlers, nodders, barkers and jesters. They are soft tissue wrapped around brittle bones and they have no training in the art of pain. The toff looks into my eyes and for the first time he can see the scary truth: when Jesus was handing out the crazy, I joined the line more than once.

The lookout whistles. The spectators split and dissolve in different directions. The damp dealer grabs the two other cards and quickly turns on his heel. It's just the toff, the money, the card, and me. I turn it over and of course, it isn't the Queen of Hearts. When I look back up the toff is gone, carried away on his worn-out shoes through the worn-out crowd.

The card is the Ace of Diamonds. Yeah. Paddy got a red one.

13

FREEDOM

FRIDAY, JUNE 8, 1979

I'd sworn never to seek assistance from my Uncle Joe, and yet I was knocking on the door of his flat, looking for a place to stay.

"Sorry about the mother, lovely woman," he said, then almost immediately followed up with, "So, the girlfriend dumped you and fucked off to France? They're all the same. Cunts."

Uncle Joe liked to tell people he'd arrived in London "the same time as the Beatles". But UncleJoemania had never taken off and the Fab 1 was angry most of the time. His marriage had ended and he'd found himself stuck in a tiny room in Harlesden, made even smaller by the fact that it contained exactly half of his married possessions. Half the furniture, half the wedding gifts, half the bedding, half the towels, half the knives and forks. When I asked him about the contents of a large box at the side of his bed, he laughed like a madman. "She kept the washing machine, but I got the tumble dryer. Hah! I hope the bitch remembers me when she's walking around in wet clothes."

A two-bar electric fire remained on at all times, sucking every molecule of moisture from the air and super-heating the nylon carpet until it shriveled like dry brush on the verge of ignition. Joe himself was gradually desiccating too, shrinking into a condensed core of singular malice.

He cleared a space on the couch and told me to treat it like home. "It's great to have new blood," he said, sounding like an old vampire. Then he asked me what I wanted to do with my future.

"Well," I said, "eventually I'd like to open a shop on Oxford Street selling Irish odds and ends: knobbly shillelaghs, music-box cottages, teddy bears in green jumpers, Claddagh rings and leprechaun hats. I'll call it the 'Knick-Knack-Paddy-Shack.'"

"Do you know what?" said Joe, nodding excitedly. "If I had the money, I'd back you."

I finally realised Joe had no sense of humour whatsoever.

One of Joe's principal interests, apart from "sinking pints", was finding a raging nymphomaniac to replace his wife. He was convinced he would eventually locate one in the Greenford Catholic Club.

"We'll have to go there together," he would say. His idea was to use me as bait. "You're a good-looking young chap. They'll flock around you, and maybe old Joe will catch a bit of the overspill, if you know what I mean."

The nights were long in Joe's little room. After work, I would come home to a "tray dinner" of blackened rashers and sausages. We ate side by side, sitting on his bed, watching natural disasters unfold on the BBC. Joe was always on the lookout. Whenever he saw a young woman standing beside a devastated home in Mexico, the walls ripped apart by a typhoon, or a Filipino girl fleeing from a village set alight by volcanic ash, he would point a greasy fork at the television and pronounce: "Fine pair of knockers."

I got the sense that he was turned on as much by their homelessness as he was by their bodies. These women were within his range. He had something they would find appealing. He had a roof over his head and a tumble dryer at his bedside.

I was trying to get over Kim Sutton, but Uncle Joe wouldn't let her go. "Don't worry, there'll be a special place in hell for the whore, right beside my missus. They'll be rubbing shoulders in the nude as the devil pokes them with a fiery mickey."

Then his eyes glazed over and I could see he was lost in his own private porn movie: *Hot Lesbos in Hades*.

At the end of the second week, I began looking for other ways to fill up the evenings. The upstairs flat was occupied by Polly and her brother, Errol. She was vividly West Indian with chestnut hair wrapped in a twist of bright red ribbon. He was six-foot-six and dreadlocked, a Watusi warrior in NHS spectacles.

One evening, as Joe watched Tropical Cyclone Tony sweeping across the Indian Ocean, I slipped out of the room.

"This is a big one," I heard him say.

Errol answered the upstairs door. He wobbled and waned as the warm smell of ganja seeped out around him. Polly reclined on a sofa in a neat room decorated with family pictures and a couple of African masks. I sat between them, and Errol offered me the joint.

"Time to take some wisdom," he said.

The weed was strong and uncut with tobacco. I took three deep breaths and handed it to Polly. We drank Red Stripe and swapped stories about island life and the different paths that had brought us to NW10. I told them about the dirty river that ran through our town, poisoned by asbestos and sweetened with sulphites.

"I thought Ireland was green," said Errol. BAINTE DEN STOC

"Not just green," I replied. "Mouldy too."

Polly told us how a mongoose had bitten her when she was eleven years old, but when she examined her ankle, she couldn't find the scar.

"Rikki-Tikki-Tavi," said Errol, rolling the words around in his mouth with the ganja smoke.

"What happened to my scar?" Polly said, probing her skin with yellow-painted fingernails.

"Rikki-Tikki-Tikki-Tikki-Tavi."

The buzz was soft and mellow. Sounds blended into a muffled hum. Polly dropped a sugar cube into a tiny glass of rum, and sighed.

"I got a new song," Errol said, jumping to his feet. "This song I write is called 'Freedom'."

Polly stifled a laugh. "He can't sing," she said.

"This song," he persisted, "is a tribute to my Caribbean home."

He started to croak: *Freedom is a thing called Kingston, Jamaica. Freedom is a thing called Marcus Garvey. Freedom is a thing called Black Star Liner...*

He danced, wiggled his backside and clapped his hands. Polly stood up and wiggled her own pretty rear end.

"Freedom is a thing called shaking your bottom," she sang.

Even Errol had to laugh. He offered up his hands in surrender, and then sat back down. He took off his spectacles and wiped a tear of good humour from his eyes. Polly pinched his cheeks and called him "my big baby brother", and then she threw herself onto my lap, where she nestled and whispered, "Will you find my scar?"

"Please!" groaned Errol. "Not the appendix one."

There was a knock on the door. Errol padded across the room and opened it. Uncle Joe stood outside with a troubled expression, a shiny suit, and hair flattened with oil. He looked waterproof, like a seal. Polly invited him in but he said no, he was just calling to collect me. Apparently, we had arranged to go out. How had he managed to track me down? He shifted with embarrassment and said, "I heard voices."

"You can get medication for that," I said, but Joe's expression rejected all comedy. He scanned the situation: Polly in my lap, her hand resting on my chest; the room filled with the rich tang of narcotic; the giant black-skinned man in the red, green and gold socks. He looked worried.

Downstairs, he told me he was upset that I had not remembered our arrangement. He made the gesture of a man casting a fishing rod and hauling in a large catch.

"Women," he said. "Greenford Catholic Club."

My heart sank.

"Pints first," he said. "I know this smashing place in Kilburn."

My heart sank lower.

Hegarty's Harp was almost empty. The woman behind the counter had a spiteful face and a Leitrim accent. Joe betrayed some consternation when I ordered a "queer drink" of Bacardi and Coke and his immediate reaction was to overcompensate. "I'll have *two* pints of Guinness," he said.

At the table, he launched into a lecture about "the blacks" and the secret war they waged against us. "The West Indian black isn't the worst, but he can't be trusted. The African black, very dangerous – he's used to being shot at, so he's hard to scare. The Brazilian black is good-looking, but he always carries a weapon. Worst of them all is the black Pakistani, descended from the Bantu or the Zulu. The Brick Lane market is full of them. Never, ever buy a pair of shoes off this fella. You'll be crippled for life."

A ratty little man came to our table and shook a collection box. He had porter-stained whiskers and fingers that were creosote brown. His breath came out in pungent globs and he leaned in far too close for comfort. "For the wives and children," he said.

"Right-you-be," said Joe as he reached for his wallet, but I was confused. "Who are you collecting for?"

"The wives and children," he snapped.

"Republican prisoners," Joe whispered, tucking a pound note into the slot.

The man rattled his box in my direction, and waited.

I waited.

Joe got nervous.

Still stoned, I wondered if we could persuade this creature to invest in the Knick-Knack-Paddy-Shack. He looked like he might be in the market for a knobbly shillelagh or a miniature alarm clock with green sticks of TNT attached.

Joe dug his elbow into my ribs and the ratty man gave a hard smile that belonged behind a balaclava.

"Why didn't you say so?" I said, pulling out a fistful of coins and spilling them on the table. The man reached out a hungry paw.

"Go on," I said. "Take any one that doesn't have the queen's head on it."

The paw retracted and the ratty expression turned cartoon comic, with bulging eyes and twitching whiskers.

"I'll remember you," he said.

"That's funny," I replied, "because I've forgotten you already."

Ten minutes later, in the green glow outside Hegarty's Harp, Uncle Joe pushed me against a wall and showered me with spit.

"That man in there," he said, "is fighting for Irish freedom!"

"Freedom is a thing called shaking your bottom," I said.

Joe looked bewildered. He pounded the sides of his head with his fists. "You definitely come from the mad side of the family," he said. "There's a weak strain, and you surely picked it up."

It started to rain on Kilburn, a dirty Irish rain with particles of misery suspended in every droplet. The sodden sheet of cloud sagged on the rooftops, and I turned to walk away. Joe's mouth dropped and his eyes tightened like a hurt child.

"Ah c'mon. I wasn't serious. Where are you going? Come back. What about the women? Don't you want a woman? I want to help you forget that tramp who fucked off to France."

I kept walking. An ocean of rain plummeted from the sky and the trees bent over in the sudden gale. Joe ran after a 31 bus, but his new leather soles found no purchase on the pavement. He skittered and fell. He jumped back up and battled against the wind, leaning forward and beating it with his head. Rivulets of water lashed from his earlobes and the jet stream of air pushed his breath back down into his chest. His battle was epic and mightily fought. For all the world, he looked like a man caught in the face of a hurricane.

14

STORYTIME

'The best stories have more than one ending.'
Old Irish saying

SATURDAY, JUNE 9, 1979

Money has become my new God, my sacred cow, my cash cow. The moolah cow. Back in Ireland, I was a draughtsman in a rusty, dusty steelworks, drawing girders and joists on crisp sheets of tracing paper for twenty-five quid a week (nineteen after tax) and I was always penniless on the wrong side of Tuesday. Now, working for British Nuclear Fuels Limited, I make a pound for every person I poison with plutonium, and I just can't spend it fast enough.

I sit at a table in the Palm Court at the Ritz hotel, nibbling on a scone slathered in Cornish clotted cream, listening to a very fine fellow as he tickles the ivories and teases the ebonies. "A Nightingale Sang in Berkeley Square" is followed by polite clapping and the genteel ping of sugar tongs on fine bone china.

Overwhelmed by etiquette, I decide that in future I will substitute the word "gosh" for the word "fuck" wherever possible.

The waiter approaches. "Would sir care for more tea?"

"*Gosh*! Yes, please," I twitter.

I'm wearing the petrol-blue silk suit and a Jermyn Street shirt. If I don't let the accent slip, no one will ever suspect I'm a Paddy. As long as I don't dance a little jig and bandy my shillelagh and drag my knuckles on the floor and munch a bunch of shamrock, I might just get away with it.

To my right, a fat woman with two bored daughters and an accent dredged from the bottom of the Manchester ship canal says, "You'll be sorry if you don't enjoy yourselves." At the table beside her, a man in a striped suit signals for the waiter. His date is young and auburn. She says something that sounds like "brew", but the man in the suit corrects her and says "*Brut*." One is champagne and the other is Carlsberg. Even a Paddy knows that.

To my left, a woman in a sparkly sweater knitted from unravelled Brillo smiles at me, but I do not smile back. I am twenty years old and she must be at least thirty. Her lost virginity is buried under half a lifetime.

A heavy man and a heavier woman work their way through a stack of triangular, crust-free sandwiches. He gives his opinion on everything in a voice as thick as the clotted cream.

She says: "The cutlery is on top of the wardrobe, unopened, never been so much as taken out of the box."

"Pure waste of money," he replies.

"How long does it take to build a stairs?" she asks.

"Three days, max."

Perhaps that's her name: Max.

The sun shines through the overhead stained glass, toasting

the back of my neck. All of a sudden I'm back in 1975, and a summer job in a glasshouse.

Edmund Fitzgerald, aka "the Wreck", wiped the sweat from his forehead on an outsized handkerchief the size of a pillowcase. Johnny "Stitches" Nolan pulled on the lever that opened the roof vents, but nothing happened.

"You're wasting your time," said the Wreck. "They're cranked all the way already."

Stitches yanked the lever and the overhead panes rattled. The Wreck sat down on the floor beside me. He wasn't built for kneeling or squatting. His legs were twice as long as his torso.

"Are you all right there, Young Hendrix?"

I got my nickname from a Jimi Hendrix T-shirt I sometimes wore.

"I'm fine," I said.

Stitches sat down on the warm concrete pathway. He pried a terracotta pot free – each glasshouse contained more than a thousand such pots – and tipped it onto the rubber mat. The earth inside was bone dry and the seedlings looked like leathery prunes.

"Three!" Stitches exclaimed. He was a long way off the Wreck's record of six.

This was our job, to separate seedlings from dried clay and note the condition and number. Our employer was the embarrassingly named Potato Research Unit, a lesser division of the Agricultural Research Institute.

The clock-like thermometer on the wall approached 116 degrees Fahrenheit. Once it hit 120, we were permitted to retreat into the shade, but it never hit 120. The sweat dropped from my chin into the dirt and the dark stain disappeared almost immediately.

Both the Wreck and Stitches reeked of Guinness. It oozed out of their pores and glistened blackly on their skin. They looked and smelled like alcoholic sharks.

The thermometer registered 116 degrees.

Stitches lit a cigarette to keep away the whitefly. "Last Saturday night," he began, "I went to a dance in the hall up the hill."

"You can't dance," said the Wreck.

"Dancing isn't about dancing," said Stitches, as he grabbed a handful of smoke and flies. "I had a few large bottles in the Glenside Lounge before I headed up the hill. I wasn't jarred, but I was fortified. I had the good jacket on, the trousers ironed, the shoes polished. I was licked and smathered."

"You were like a movie star."

Stitches ignored the sarcasm. "I was indeed," he said, "but the same can't be said for the women in the hall. It was the usual mob. Lumpy girls from the Presentation Convent looking for a man with three hairs on his head and three grand in the post office. Admission was fifty pence – you'd expect something better."

"Romance?" suggested the Wreck.

"I would have settled for cleavage, but these girls were covered up like racehorses on a frosty morn. To be honest, I was ready to pack it in and be at the loss of the money, when I spotted the woman of my dreams. She was standing at the mineral bar wearing a tight red blouse and a short white miniskirt."

"In the hall up the hill?" sneered the Wreck.

Stitches nodded. "Long legs, sandals, painted toenails – and she was looking straight in my direction. I couldn't believe it."

"You're not alone."

The thermometer approached 117 degrees. Stitches upended the pot and tipped out the dirt and the seedlings.

"I hit the jackpot here," he said. "Seven."

The Wreck let out a long, stringy spit that landed on the glass and slid downwards like greasy rain. "No way, José," he said. "There's never seven in a pot. You must've snuck a few of them in."

"You saw me empty it out."

The Wreck wanted to pursue the matter, but there was something else on his mind. "We'll come back to this later on," he said. "Right now I want to hear what happened with the woman."

"Ah yes," Stitches said as he wrote up the score in his notebook. "You want me to continue."

"I don't believe a word that comes out of that mouth," said the Wreck, "but I do need something to distract me from this heat."

We all looked at the thermometer. It registered 117 degrees.

"Well," Stitches continued, "your woman comes right over. She takes my hand and brings me outside. She leads me up that little boreen that ends beside the slate quarry."

"I know the place," said the Wreck, spitting once more on the glass.

"We stopped and looked out at the valley and the towns below, floating like three shiny trout on a black pond."

"Were you touching her?" asked the Wreck, pulling out his handkerchief and mopping his brow.

"I had my arm around her shoulders."

"That's not what I meant."

The thermometer was stuck at 117 degrees.

Stitches drifted off into a magic place, a night-world filled with sparkly dust. He described the warmth of the air and the fragrance it carried. He spoke at length about the stillness and the quiet. "Not a car nor a wobbly bicycle anywhere in the world, but there was a glow beyond the horizon, thousands of miles away. It might have been New York, or maybe Las Vegas."

Beyond our glass ceiling, the sky was Egyptian blue. Two women in lab coats cycled past, chatting and laughing. I recognized one of them. She was the farm manager's daughter, a girl with the wrong face on a decent body. She had studied me with longing in the recreation room, but then I'd beaten her mercilessly at table tennis.

The world is full of unwanted desire.

"Did you TOUCH her?" bellowed the Wreck.

"You're very crude," said Stitches.

"Tell me there's more to this story than moonlight and the scent of wild fucking honeysuckle."

A cloud of whitefly descended. It was my turn to light a cigarette and keep them at bay.

"Good man, Young Hendrix," said Stitches.

The thermometer slipped back to 116 degrees. The Wreck cursed as he unbuttoned his white shirt. Stitches emptied a small bottle of tap water over the back of his head.

The tale, unfinished, hung suspended.

The two young women dismounted their bicycles. They stood on the bank of the ornamental lake and watched the lazy swans. The farm manager's daughter tried not to look at me, but she couldn't resist. Our eyes met through the glass and the greasy spit trails, just for an instant, until she remembered 21-3, the final score in the table tennis game. She turned her plain face away. We were dead to each other.

The Wreck slapped a horsefly and smeared it on his arm. He left it there, a warning to others. He upended a pot and shook out the dirt. There were no seedlings. He didn't care. "For fuck's sake Stitches, finish the story."

"Isn't that what I'm doing?"

"Tell me you dropped the hand. If we get to the end of this story and it turns out you never dropped the hand, I'll be dropping you."

Stitches lowered his voice, concerned that the young women might hear us through the glass. The Wreck leaned in closer.

I studied the two men. Stitches' head was like a red bowling ball made for small fingers. When he wasn't speaking, which was rare, his lips relaxed into an "O" shape. He looked like he was perpetually on the verge of saying "obviously". The Wreck resembled an unwashed root vegetable. He had been working with the spuds too long, and now he was part-tuber himself. Soon he would put down roots in the glasshouse and he would learn to love the sun. He would stop fighting the whitefly.

"What are you smiling at, Young Hendrix?" Stitches asked.

"Nothing," I said.

"The woman!" growled the Wreck. "I want to know about the woman."

The girls mounted their bicycles and rode past us. The farm manager's daughter focused on a spot just beyond oblivion, and pedalled towards it.

"That woman," Stitches continued, "was hotter than a Christian Brother's strap. She pulled me into a gateway on the old boreen. She put her arms around my neck and her tongue in my mouth."

"Get away!" said the Wreck.

"She was wrapped around me, like a dirty blanket on a tinker."

The poetry was gone and with it the illusion of wonder and mystery. Stitches and the Wreck were alive in a moment that never was. A two man tug-of-war, the rope of truth stretched to breaking point between them.

"How does it end?" asked the Wreck.

"I'll tell you how it ends," replied Stitches.

The waiter puts a fresh pot of tea on the table. He knows I'm a fake. We're all fakes in the Palm Court: the heavy-set couple and the Brillo lady; the Manchester woman and her two daughters; the stripe-suited man and his teenage date. Fake and fake. The real aristocracy wouldn't touch this place with a barge pole. Their meetings and dealings are conducted in a parallel world beyond view, dipped in claret and shrouded in Cohiba smoke. Afternoon tea at the Ritz is for the bumpkins: solicitors, both legal and sexual; shady builders and their lacquered wives. It's a place where Paddies go to laugh at the world, to say, "Four years ago I was a farm labourer with a brown bicycle and a plaid thermos flask, but look at me now, Ma. I'm on top of the world."

"How does it end?" asked the Wreck.

In the winter of 1976, Stitches Nolan stepped out of the Four Counties pub after a substantial feed of Guinness. He walked a mile on the middle of the road before he was hit by an oncoming car. The driver tried to resuscitate him, to breathe life into that mouth with its strange circular shape, but Stitches was dead.

Obviously.

A few months later, they found the Wreck in his cottage, the fire burned out in the grate and a neat bundle of empty pay packets resting on the mantle; he had saved nothing, and nothing could save him. His liver and heart got together and killed him. He lay on a lonely bed, a cloud of flies hovering overhead.

In death, as in life.

"I'll tell you how it ends," replied Stitches. "She took my hand and she put it up her skirt."

"Go 'way," said the Wreck, his eyes as big as poker chips. "Go 'way to fuck."

"I swear," Stitches said, crossing his heart. "She took that hand there and she pushed it right up her mini."

"What was it like?" asked the Wreck, his poker-chip eyes doubling in value.

"I'll tell you now, not a word of a lie, what I found up there gave me a shock I will never forget."

The Wreck blinked. His face hardened. His lips trembled. He looked like a man who had just received very bad news. "For Christ's sake, Stitches. We've all heard this story before, or at least some variation of it."

"What are you trying to say?" asked Stitches. "You don't believe me?"

"Of course I don't fucking believe you. And what's more, I'm insulted."

"Why would you be insulted?"

"I'm insulted because everybody knows what happens when a man such as yourself meets an unexpected beauty in a rural dancehall and takes her out to a quiet spot for a bit of the old holy rosary. You get your hand in that place where it shouldn't be, and what do you find? She isn't a woman at all. She's a man! It's as fucking hackneyed as they come."

Stitches shook his head in total disagreement. He was hurt, shocked, dismayed. "No, no, no," he said in a soft whisper. "She wasn't a man, definitely not. No, nay, never."

"THEN WHAT WAS SHE?" roared the Wreck.

Stitches looked left and right and over both shoulders before he revealed the dreadful mystery.

"She was a robot," he said.

I thought the Wreck would have a seizure. His eyes popped and his chin dropped. He upended the wheelbarrow full of clay. He stumbled and cracked a pot with his boot. His elbow banged against a pane and almost went through it. He cursed. He spat on the glass. He summoned a power from the middle of his weighty gut, an orgasm of amazement that tore up his spine and rippled into his muscular shoulders. He doubled over, slapped his knees and then laughed until his cheeks turned puce.

Stitches made things worse by remaining impassive, yet puzzled. With hands on hips and head tilted to one side, he was a statue erected to integrity, a sculpted block of veracity. He had told a lie so perfect it could only be the truth, and he was proud of it.

The girls on the bicycles probably heard the laughter, but they didn't look back. The manager's daughter may have thought it was directed at her, that her passion had become a source of hot-house amusement, a joke among sweat-soaked men. She may have blushed furiously as she rang her little bell on the road to oblivion, but her back was turned and her shapely rear revealed nothing.

Stitches could only keep it in for so long. Eventually he had to let go. He cracked wide open and his O-shaped mouth turned ovoid in joy. He punched the Wreck on the shoulder and the Wreck punched him back. They giggled like schoolgirls until the tears ran down their cheeks.

"A robot!" said the Wreck.

"A robot!" repeated Stitches.

The temperature fell to 115, but neither man noticed. A small cloud headed towards the sun and the swans raised their wings, pretending to fly.

This is how it ends.

15

RENT

SUNDAY, JUNE 24, 1979

Carla held down the smoke for so long, all that came out was a barely visible contrail of shimmering air. Before leaving Buenos Aires, she had been a swimmer and a dancer; her lungs probably ran the length of her body. I pictured her in a tarlatan tutu, doing *grand plié* and *arabesque*. I imagined her emerging from the back of a black Mercedes at the gates of the Teatro Colón, as the other ballerinas looked on with envy. A child of wealth, she spoke four languages and rode a horse like a seasoned gaucho, but she was already lost.

"Are you thinking about your girlfriend?"

I said no, even though I was.

"What's on your mind?" she asked, handing back the glass pipe.

"Our worlds," I said, and she knew I meant the vast space between them.

I had seen a photograph that showed her poised at the end of an aquamarine pool, a lofty mansion towering behind her. She had a yawn on her lips and a dullness in her eyes. She was bored by a life the rest of us could barely imagine.

"Tell me about yours," she said.

When I was young, I swam in a cold Irish river. The outlet pipe from the nearby sugar factory pumped warmth and sweetness into a swirling school of fat little fish. Once, after a heavy shower of rain, a dead sheep flipped over at the weir and exposed a burst belly and a trailing spiral of guts. In my river there were more suicides than swimmers.

I remember the town clerk standing at the front of our classroom with a balsa model of a proposed community pool. "If every child in the county could give two shillings," he said in a small voice, filling the pool with water from a Lucozade bottle. Then he turned his fingers into a running man, hopped on the diving board and flipped into the deep end. Finally he lifted off the roof of the girls changing room and granted us a look at a mesmerising world of miniature femininity. The Christian Brother at the top of the classroom was not impressed.

We all donated our shillings, but the pool never came. Our dream of vaulting and twisting from that diving board, plummeting like shot game into the shimmering blue – it was just a dream that would never be wet.

"So sad," Carla said, replacing the pipe on the chair beside the bed. We watched the narcotic tar as it continued to glow. She smiled in the dim light and arched her back. The line of dots on her arm looked like spider bites. "You have a beautiful body," she whispered. My body was exactly like hers: thin and twenty and wasted. She ran a pointed red fingernail down my bare chest, as if she were about to unzip the flesh. "I knew this would happen the first day I opened the door and saw you standing there."

Three weeks previously, outside the Criterion on Piccadilly Circus, I'd bumped into Noel Reddy, excited and red-faced. He wasn't really a school pal. Our desks had once touched, but our paths had never crossed.

"McKinley! Fuck! It is you. I saw you going past. I knew it was you, but you've lost weight haven't you?" He stood back and examined me. "You're not sick, are you?"

Maybe I should have told him I was dying of something contagious and consumptive, but he looked lonely, and lonely people are hard to scare away. We went for a drink in the back bar at the Black Heart. It was a resting spot where the Dilly boys paused between clients and used the bitter ale for mouthwash.

When Noel discovered I had nowhere to stay, he was excited. "Do you remember Sheila Nolan from back home?" he asked.

"No."

"She lived on the terrace?"

"No."

"She had long red-brown hair?"

"No."

"Her father worked for C.I.E.?"

"Still no."

"Her brother was up in court for setting fire to a cat?"

"Ahh! Right," I said, vaguely remembering a headline.

"She's living not that far from here and she's looking for somebody to share."

"Share what?"

"The flat! Just off Oxford Street. Jesus. Great location, plus she has a hot-looking friend from Argentina. Maybe they're lesbians. You think she likes pussy?"

"Well if she does," I said, "she's one step up on her brother."

Gloucester Place, later that day. I looked over the railing and down to the basement flat. The curtains were drawn. I rang the bell and a skinny boy in a pair of baggy underpants answered the door. I asked him whether Sheila was around, but he smiled and said, "I only speak seven words in English." Behind him, a woman's voice called out, "Do you know what time it is?"

"If you're an actress or a hooker," I said, "you don't need to get up yet."

A dark-haired girl in a full-length nightdress came to the door.

"I'm both," she said with a smirk. "I'm Carla and this is Paolo."

"I only speak seven words in English," he repeated.

She turned back into the room and spoke loudly. "There is a thin young man here. Do you want him?"

Sheila appeared, barefoot and wrapped in an oversize rugby jersey.

"You seem vaguely familiar," she said. "Do you know my brother?"

"Meow!" I replied.

She stifled a laugh, then looked back over her shoulder nervously. "He's staying with us for the weekend. He's still asleep. What's your name?"

"McKinley."

"Barry McKinley?"

I nodded.

"Oh my God, yes!" she said. "You're from home – you were in the Regional College. You used to be gorgeous."

"Yeah," I said. "Shame what happened to me."

"No, no, no. You're still gorgeous but it's just... you lost weight, didn't you?"

I asked if she needed another flatmate and she nodded. "The rent here is sixty quid a week and we never have it."

"If you're sleeping in the afternoon," I said, "you shouldn't be surprised by poverty."

"You could have the bedroom for thirty a week."

She allowed me to slide past her in the doorway and I could smell the sleep rising from her skin. We picked our way through the wreckage of empty beer cans, torn Rizla packets and ashtrays stacked like butt-filled towers of babel. A body stirred in a sleeping bag on the floor. Paolo sat at the cluttered table and rolled a joint. He smiled and said, "I only speak seven words in English." He looked like a happy kid.

Sheila led me under a low arch. I ducked and when I came back up, I was in the "bedroom". The basement had once been a kitchen servicing the house upstairs, and this alcove was the coal cellar. There was an iron manhole cover directly above our heads.

"This is it," she said. "It's actually quite comfortable."

"Yeah," I replied, "assuming they don't deliver two ton of anthracite."

"I'll need two weeks' rent in advance," she said.

I looked around and saw a bookshelf that held a dozen cheap novels and a Chianti bottle covered in melted wax. When I looked back, Sheila was staring at me. She had hardly any inhibitions. London can do that to a young Irish girl.

"You really are gorgeous," she said.

"I know."

She shouted something in Italian to Paolo and he replied with a "*mucho bello*".

"He thinks you're cute."

"Should I be changing the lock on the bedroom door?"

"We're very bohemian around here. Almost anything goes."

I gave her the deposit and later that evening, when I returned with a suitcase, the killer of cats was gone. Paolo was dressed, but

Sheila and Carla were much as I'd left them. A surly Italian called Arturo had joined them and all four were playing Scopa with a 40-card deck. When I asked for a key, Sheila said, "We never lock the door."

"You could have the necks cutted in the night," said Arturo in damaged English, but Sheila shrugged and laid a Cavallo on the table. She told me the flat belonged to a pair of Lebanese brothers referred to as "The Brilliantined Levantines". They lived upstairs and sometimes they sat on the windowsills with their legs dangling over Montagu Place. Their eyes rolled with the passing of women. "They watch everything," she said.

That first night, we exchanged stories about our lives, some fact, some fiction, the two winding together in a helix of smoky bravado. Arturo worked in a shirt shop on the King's Road and had once measured David Bowie's neck. Paolo showed us a road map of Sicily and pointed to a small town in the hills. Sheila stared at me as she gave a brief lesson in the Irish language she had learned as a child.

"*Teigh a chodladh a linbh.*"

"What does it mean?" asked Carla.

"Baby, go to sleep."

Carla yawned and lay down on the mattress by the window. She told us about the schools that had rejected her, from Torino to Lucerne and finally somewhere cold and posh in the Cotswolds. Her expulsion papers always said the same thing. She was "incompatible" with the other young women, and might perhaps be "happier elsewhere". You only had to look at the spider bites on her arm to know that she would never be happy anywhere.

The days rolled past and the weather grew hot. The door stood wide open most of the time. Flies buzzed in, circled, and left.

Arturo never returned and Paolo did not learn another word of English.

One evening I came home and found Carla and Sheila giggling at the table. "We drew cards to see which of us would shag you," said Sheila, tapping three short stacks of playing cards. "We took turns drawing from the deck until one of us pulled the Jack of Hearts."

"You really do have too much time on your hands." I took a Rothmans from the table, and a thought struck me. "*Three* piles?"

"Well, we could hardly leave Paolo out of the competition," said Sheila matter-of-factly.

In the bedroom, I lay down and burned some poppy gum in a bowl. Looking around, I realised I had not left much of a mark. The small suitcase beside the bed contained toiletries, underwear and a packet of Rizla: everything I needed for permanent exile. I could walk out with all that I owned and still have a free hand to hail a taxi.

Carla knocked on the door and came in. I pulled myself upright on the bed, because only the Buddha and lingerie models look good lying down.

"Don't get up," she said, displaying the Jack of Hearts.

"You won the competition?"

"No. *You* won," she replied. "Are you disappointed?"

"I'm relieved it's not Paolo."

We fell on the tired springs and her cool white body settled upon me like a feather.

"Our worlds," I said, and I could see the pale blue swimming pool reflected in her eyes. She folded her arms into the butterfly stroke and dived right into me. She touched bottom and came back up for air. We splashed, surged and rolled around. We grappled, drowned, and resuscitated one another. Mouth upon mouth. Breast upon chest.

"Our worlds," I said again.

I didn't know that three days later I would come home and find her gone, the flat in darkness, the silence thick and unexpected. Nor could I have predicted the hand hooking me from the blackness, swinging me to the floor.

"Our worlds," she whispered back.

I did not foresee the Brilliantined Levantines standing above me, shouting down, "Where is the whore, the queer and the junkie?" as they took turns stepping on my fingers. "Where is six weeks' rent? Three hundred quid? Somebody pay!" The empty wallet pulled from my pocket. More kicks and curses in a foreign tongue, a trickle of blood and a searing pain. Pages torn from a passport, ripped and sprinkled like green confetti. Finally, the angry brothers drifting out the door like a scented Mediterranean breeze.

"*Teigh...*" said Carla, as she took one last hit from the pipe.

" *... a chodladh a linbh*," I finished, as I rolled from her body.

Three days later, Carla would settle herself into a first-class seat on a 747, bound for Ezeiza Airport. Sheila and Paolo would spend the last of my money on chicken kebabs and train tickets to Holyhead. And I would stand in The Black Heart, surrounded by the painted Polari pansies and the thirsty queers with beers. I would be gorgeous, broken and homeless; tired, stoned and unattainable; another pretty face in a sea of wanton wasters. I would be the rent boy who didn't have the rent.

16

MOON

FRIDAY, JULY 13, 1979

My boss cornered me outside his office and said, "Uh, uh... Barry..."

In my experience conversations that started with "uh, uh... Barry..." seldom ended well.

"I've caught a few mistakes," said Chris Longley, waving about my drawing of the contamination containment area in Windscale/Sellafield. "Minor stuff – don't be too concerned. It's not the end of the world."

Early days yet, I thought.

"Actually," he continued, "my sister, she, um, gave me these tickets for the theatre tonight and..."

"I would love to go to the theatre with you," I said, though I would have preferred to stuff a live badger in my pants.

"It's an Irish play..." he blurted out.

Make that two live badgers.

I suggested we meet in Ward's Irish House, Piccadilly. This was part of a grand plan to make sure he never asked me out again. Ward's had once been a public convenience attached to the London Underground; now it was a basement warren full of foul-smelling nooks and a circular bar where insane Paddies stared at one other until somebody screamed, "Who-da-fuck-are-ye-lookin'-at?"

I arrived early and stood beside a Mayo man with a mop of tangled hair and a jumper that had been chewed by farm animals. He watched my every movement through the side of his eye and when I ordered a Bacardi, his face was seized by a muscular spasm.

"... and Coke."

Bowels all around the counter loosened.

"Oh yes," said the Mayo man to himself. "Oh yes indeed."

I looked at him and he looked away. "Oh yes," he said. "Oh yes indeed."

A trip to the gents was revolting but necessary. The mirror was cracked, the taps were filthy and the floor was stickier than contact cement. I popped a couple of mauve tablets and looked at the face in the fractured mirror. "Oh yes," I said. "Oh yes indeed."

Back in the bar, the Mayo man had been joined by a sheep-shagger from Gweedore and a speed-talker from Dundalk. Their conversation sounded like dog language: all yelps and throaty growls.

Twenty minutes later, Chris Longley came tap dancing down the stairs, out of breath and red-faced, flapping like a runaway turkey. The sheep-shagger raised his eyebrows and the speed-talker let out a burst of noise that sounded like a trumpet fanfare. I took Chris Longley into the corner booth known as "The Munster Room".

"I'm dreadfully sorry," he said. "My bus was delayed."

He lit a Rothmans and began to smoke in short bursts of action, like an escaped mental patient. The men at the bar watched him. Somebody muttered, "He'd look good on me mantelpiece."

Chris Longley studied the acres of Irish kitsch lining the narrow shelves: old hurling trophies and leather-bound books, the one un-cleaned and the other unopened. Postcards from Sligo and rusty horseshoes, hung upside down with the luck running out.

"I like this place," he said. "I might come back here, just pop in myself sometime."

"That could be dangerous," I said.

"Really?"

He didn't understand. There were places in England where the English weren't welcome, from the dingy shebeens in Cricklewood to the Rasta bookies on Brixton Road. Free trade zones where the rules of Empire would never apply.

Chris Longley's drink arrived and he said "Slawn-Cha". Oblivious to the grunts of laughter, he took a small sip and the little crescent of cream on his lip straightened before he licked it away.

"Dashed good," he said.

It was clear that he had no idea how dangerous it was to use a word like "dashed" in an Irish bar. It was up there with "gosh," "by jove!" and "where did we leave the Bentley, Smithers?"

He lowered his voice and leaned towards me. "I have a little surprise," he said.

This was definitely the wrong place to pull out a bunch of flowers and an engagement ring.

"I'm putting you in charge of systems in the handling facility."

I looked into his eyes and wondered what was wrong with him. On any given day I had more drugs in my system than the entire Chinese swimming team. I needed to be given the boot, not promotion.

"You would be dealing with grade 'A' *matériel*," he said,

referring to six hundred and fifty tons of graphite riven with 1,000 radioactive rods. "It's all high-level top-notch stuff. I'll bet you're thrilled," he said.

"Thrilled" was another word best left unused in an Irish setting. I said I was happy, and looked round at the hunchback Paddies. They hadn't heard, but they would have been impressed. I was now in charge of the biggest bomb on the British mainland: a giant keg of Strontium, Caesium and Rhodium with a fuse of human stupidity, connected to a battery of dodgy narcotics. With one crooked stroke of a pencil, I could wipe out Western Europe. A simple skewing of dimensions and the edge of the continent would light up like flash paper in a panto. I was so lost in the power of the moment that I failed to hear Chris Longley when he asked his question, so he asked it again.

"Why don't you drink Guinness?"

The huddled Micks turned and tuned their ears like something at Jodrell Bank. There was total silence as everyone awaited the answer.

It was time to tell the story of Jimmy Moon.

"I was five years old," I began, "living in a big old house in the Irish countryside. An impossibly tall wall surrounded the cottage next door and strange noises sometimes drifted over the top. It was hard to tell if they were animal or human. I remember one afternoon playing close to the wall, when I became aware of a shadow cast over me. I looked up and saw a big round face with eyes like small dark buttons. It was a boy, a year or two older than me. I asked him what he was standing on because he seemed quite high up, but his expression never changed.

"'What's your name?' I asked.

"He tilted his head, blinked his eyes and made a noise not unlike the noise a cow might make. 'Mmmmmooooooon,' he said.

"'That's not a name,' I replied.

"He disappeared down behind the wall.

"'What is your name?'

"'Mmmmmmooooooon!' he shouted back, and I had the sense that he was mocking me. I found an old copper penny in a dirty puddle. It had the hen on one side and the harp on the other. I picked it up and threw it over the wall.

"'What's your name?' I demanded once again.

"Moments later, the penny came buzzing back, along with the reply, 'Mmmmmoooooon!!'

"I picked up the penny again and fired it, launching it high into the air. It turned small and dark, just like the other boy's eyes, before dropping back to earth. It didn't hit earth; it hit something else. It made the unmistakable noise of metal cracking against bone, probably a skull.

"'Aaaaaaaaahhhh,' cried a voice in pain.

"'Hello!' I said, panicking a bit. 'Hello?' But there was no reply. Feet scurried away. A door slammed. I never saw the young boy again.

"About a year ago, I ended up in a rough pub in the Rainy Town. I'd never been in there before. It was all spit, sawdust, and men with troubles. I noticed there was an awkward young man sitting at a table in the corner by himself. He wore a heavy overcoat and his head was half-turned to face the wall. His cheek bulged because he was sucking on something, maybe a boiled sweet or a gobstopper. He reminded me very much of that boy from the other side of the wall. I called over the owner of the pub, a grumpy man with eyebrows like centipedes running for the cover of his fringe.

"'Who is that chap over there?' I asked.

"'That's Jimmy Moon.'

"'Did he ever live on Green Lane?'

"'No.'

"The owner walked back down to the other end of the counter and pulled the cap off a large bottle of Smithwick's ale. He placed the bottle in front a cadaverous man, then returned.

"'But there was a woman who minded troublesome children and she used to live up on the Green Lane. She minded Jimmy from time to time. The mother would send him away from her on nights of the full moon.'

"I didn't understand.

"'Fuckin' moon used to drive him crazy. Poor woman wouldn't be able to handle him, so every month she'd give him out to different ould wans. Hard women, most of them.'

"'Is he better now?' I asked.

"'Indeed and he is not,' the owner said, 'I have him barred from the premises when *ould Selene* is complete in the heavens. I've told him to go elsewhere, but there's nowhere else that would have him. He'd be up on the tables, lepping about, calling out like a cockerel. You couldn't have that.'

"I drank my pint and ordered another. Jimmy sipped from his glass, not looking around at anyone and the thing in his mouth, whatever it was, kept moving inside his cheek, as if it were alive.

"Eventually I had to go to the gents, which was nothing more than a dark shed out in the back yard. When I returned, Jimmy was gone. His empty bottle stood alone on the table. The clock hit eleven and the owner threw a dishcloth over the bar taps.

"'Time!' he roared, 'Time NOW!'

"I swallowed a mouthful of stout, but I could hear something rattling in the glass. I emptied the dregs into a tin ashtray. At the very bottom, almost hiding in a corner of white foam, it jingled as it slid out..."

Chris stared at me with wide eyes as the literal and metaphorical penny dropped. "He'd been carrying it around, all that time, in his ...?" He couldn't even say the word "mouth". He pushed his glass away on the table.

I opened my wallet and produced an old Irish coin. You had to look close, otherwise it could have been a worn-out copper washer. The hen was mostly missing and only a couple of strings on the harp remained. I laid the penny on the counter and every man looked at it in awe.

"Come on," I said to Chris. "We'll be late for the show."

Nobody grunted or chuckled when we left because Jimmy Moon was in their midst: his haunted eyes; the rolling lump in his cheek; the angry old women with sticks and dirty fingernails who mocked a face too blank to show pain; the locked doors and boarded windows; and the slim beams of moonlight he tried to catch between his fingers. Nobody would dare touch the penny on the counter. Nobody would raise a glass or bid a sarcastic farewell to the "foreigners".

There was nothing behind us but silence as we clambered up the steps, into the mob of Piccadilly.

17

THEREMIN

Before Kim Sutton, I had a brief relationship with a German girl. Her name was Sofia. She had long legs and a short green dress and she made young men disappear in a puff of sexual uncertainty. I met her at an "Up with People" gathering, which was ironic because I didn't give a fuck about people and whether they were up or down.

"You have beautiful eyes," she said.

She was seventeen years old. Her father was the manager of a local factory that made hair dryers from bright orange plastic. She told me about the art of non-contact stimulation. Apparently it was possible to play the clitoris like a theremin. Not coming from a musical family, I found this disturbing.

"I have a key to a room in the River House," she said.

The River House was an old Georgian building in the middle of town, next to the bridge. It was home to a group of longhairs who played tambourines and penny whistles late at night. On the outside, it looked like a den seething with narcotics and perversity, but it was just a sad place with unwashed dishes in the sink and piles of hopelessness stacked against the walls.

It was after two o'clock in the morning when we got to the River House. She led me into a room with an Easy Rider poster and three ragged jumpers hooked on a door. There was a single bed, pushed tight into an alcove as if it were hiding, afraid of the weight that would test its tired springs. We got undressed. The moonlight bounced off the river and reflected waves rippled across the ceiling. Our skin was cool and blue.

I slid under the bedclothes and got to work on the theremin, but my mind was somewhere else. Irish teenagers are always dreaming of London. We imagine a city made up of connected record sleeves, from that Soho cul-de-sac of Ziggy Stardust, to the Vauxhall shop where Ian Dury stands like an outdoor mannequin. From the Camden steps of The Clash, to the Primrose Hill of the Rolling Stones. The riotous Lewisham of Sham '69; the Small Faces on Hampstead Heath; The Kinks in Waterloo Station, and The Jam on the platform at Liverpool Street.

Irish boys and girls head for London the same way that salmon head upstream. There's something that pulls us across the waves and into the swirling pool of promiscuity, a giant magnet buried under Westminster Bridge that tugs relentlessly at the iron in our souls.

Sofia's thighs were muffling my ears, so it was a while before I realised she was speaking. I surfaced into the chilly room like a U-boat rising. Her voice was low, the tone intense. At first, it seemed to be the pornographic chitchat that women think men want, and men want women to want, but then I listened closely.

She was telling me about a particular incident, about torn clothing and bruised skin.

"He ripped my skirt. He tore my underwear." A hand had covered her mouth. A knee had forced her legs apart – "like this," she said, driving a knee between my legs. She'd wanted to scream but couldn't. "He put a hand over my mouth. Like this." She took my hand and covered her lips. I could feel the words bubbling out from between the open fingers, but still I didn't understand. "Don't hurt me. Please don't hurt me. Please don't." She put her knee between my legs once more, but with extra force. "Like this," she said with urgency. "Like this!"

In the pale blue light, I looked into her eyes and tried to decipher the jumble. Who was this man? When had it happened and why was she telling me?

She repeated the sentences again. Ripped skirt: check. Torn panties: check. Mouth covered, hand on throat, failed scream attempt: check, check and check.

"Don't hurt me. Please don't hurt me. Please don't."

Something basic had changed in her voice. These were not the details from a past event. They were instructions, directives, a shopping list of assault. This was an event that had yet to happen, that was about to happen, and I was the one ordained.

"You understand?" she said. "You must understand!"

Her eyes were fierce and her theremin hummed. The room got smaller and the bed was a nervous wreck.

"You understand?"

I said I did. I put my hand on her throat and felt the air moving behind the skin. Her mouth opened but nothing came out. I lay upon her, a shroud with a face. My tongue slid into her mouth like a butcher's thumb into a carcass and I felt our teeth grate together as I sucked the wind from her lungs. She struggled and squirmed. I placed a knee between her legs and forced them open and her words rolled out in a long, soft purr.

"Don't hurt me, please don't hurt me, please don't."

I started grunting and barking out disconnected oaths and embarrassing obscenities. I sounded like a stand-up comedian, except I wasn't standing up and the words were not funny. I probed and invaded and she resisted and twisted. Probe, invade, resist and twist. Repeat, until done. Until empty.

Dennis Hopper and Peter Fonda rode their panhead Harleys above our heads into the heart of Monument Valley. They didn't look down at the shameful scene, the spent lust and the oozing mess of the moment. They didn't care about the dirty room and the broken bed. They were on their way to Mardi Gras and a date with a redneck shotgun.

I crept from the River House in the last tired moments before daylight. A drunken man with a greasy ball of newspaper in his fist staggered past, leaving a trail of limp chips and deep-fried fish on the pavement. Hearing me talk to myself, he looked back in unsteady alarm. What was I saying?

"Don't hurt me. Please don't hurt me. Please don't".

Out in the cold birth of daylight I didn't like the sound of the words. The first torments of uncertainty rattled inside my head. Had I misunderstood? Had I misread the signs? Was this a wanted act, or a wanton act? She had begged me to do it, hadn't she? I replayed her voice, trying to hear it just the right way, but I knew that in any court of law it wouldn't sound good. I pictured a judge with a gavel the size of a fairground mallet.

"What do you have to say for yourself before I send you down, down, DOWN?"

I got home and crawled into bed but the sweat came in alarming bursts and I couldn't sleep. Every time I closed my eyes, I heard that voice and those shocking words. I imagined a German girl's finger in a telephone dial, swirling all the way round, three times.

Nine, nine nine. *Nein, nein, nein.*

Who would ever believe the truth about the muffling thighs and the mixed signals? The whole thing was absurd.

At 9 a.m. I got out of bed and went back to the River House. I stood outside and watched, but nothing stirred. The windows were lifeless eyes. I wanted to knock on the door, but I imagined a horde of hippies chasing me through the streets, waving fists and tambourines.

I went to The Auld Triangle because I knew it would be quiet and dark and soothing, a library for layabouts. I put money in a slot and the balls came rumbling out. I racked them and leaned over the table. I sighted down the length of the cue, at the cluster of red, but I couldn't strike. I just stayed in that position with my cheek pressed against the baize. I imagined ten years in prison and ape-like men pulling at my body, searching for pleasure.

"Don't hurt me. Please don't hurt me. Please don't."

When I heard Sofia's voice, I thought I was dreaming, but I looked up and there she was.

"I followed you." she said. "I saw you outside the house."

I was ready for her anger, prepared for the accusations. I saw her hand coming towards me and I didn't try to dodge it. I wanted her nails to dig into my flesh. I needed to feel her knuckles punch my nose and blacken my eyes because absolution demanded bruises and blood. Every Catholic boy knows that.

Her fingers went instead for my hair and combed it backwards. The golden glow from the overhead lamp highlighted my features. I noted her expression was tender, her face more beautiful than I'd remembered. She looked straight at me and studied the emptiness within.

"I was right," she said.

"About what?"

"You do have beautiful eyes."

18

OH

The play was even worse than I'd expected. A murky stage draped with fishing nets and an upturned currach. Every now and then, a sonorous Mick pranced onto the boards and cursed the Irish skies. The rain never stopped and the cast was bedraggled and drenched.

At the intermission, I drank a Bacardi and Chris Longley ordered a cup of tea. He genuinely did. What is it with the Brits? The Zulus might be attacking but you'd still hear the sound of a whistling kettle rising above the war cries.

"What do you think?" asked Chris Longley.

"It's fabulous," I said, because when you went to the theatre you had to use at least one queer word. He sipped his tea and nodded. He ate exactly half his digestive biscuit, to indicate satisfaction, but not over-indulgence. He dusted the crumbs from his fingertips and touched the corners of his mouth with a tissue.

Where were the Zulus when you needed them?

"Is there anything better than live theatre?" he asked, and I immediately thought of the Sex Pistols. People can say whatever they want about the Kingsmen, Sonics, Mysterians, MC5 and early Underground, but until *Anarchy in the UK*, it was all just so much amplified twang. The Pistols released four singles and one album. They blew into the scene in 1976 and by late '77 they were history. They were gone, and they knew they were gone. Theatre, on the other hand, refuses to accept its own demise. It's been lying in a grave for 2,000 years, but every time you throw down a shovel of dirt, the bastard sits back up and soliloquises.

"Fabulous," he said

"Fabulous," I repeated.

The end-of-intermission bell rang and I felt like a punch-drunk boxer returning to the ring. We took our seats and watched a lone drummer limp across the stage, rapping out a beat on a bodhran while the sky turned portentous black. Chris Longley pressed his shoulder against mine and, hidden by the darkness, I stuffed a Percocet into my mouth.

After the play, we shambled onto Shaftesbury Avenue with a thousand confused Brits. To them, the island next door was more enigmatic than ever. A place to send your soldiers, but never your tourists.

"I know this great Indian restaurant in Soho," said Chris, and the night I'd thought was over had only just begun. The Taj was upscale, full of chrome and mirrors rather than brass and flock wallpaper. The waiters wore sharp suits and white turbans that looked like crash helmets made from giant onions.

"You really must tell me more about your country," Chris said, so I invented the Ireland of his imagination, full of picturesque nonsense, thatched cottages, fiddle players at crossroads, one-room schoolhouses presided over by unshaven Latin scholars.

I was tempted to throw in a leprechaun or two, but somehow managed to resist.

"Enchanting," he said.

"Enchanting," I repeated, using the second queer word of the night. I dreaded to think what the third might be. Radical action was called for. I reached into a pocket and pulled out a block of hash. "Do know what this is?"

"Yes I do," said Chris Longley, looking frantically about the restaurant. "When I was in college it was offered, but I never said yes."

"Now is your chance to say yes." I cut the cube in two and slid his portion across the tablecloth, leaving a brown smudge on the linen. He quickly covered it with his hand.

"You want to smoke this, here?" he said.

"Who said anything about smoking?"

I popped the block into my mouth, chewed and swallowed.

After some embarrassed hesitation, he picked up his half and did likewise. Our meals arrived on brass platters and a man with an onion head spooned riced onto the plates. Chris dipped his fork and put it to his lips.

"Mmm, *c'est piquant.*"

Piquant? I felt an overwhelming need to do something heterosexual, like scrimshaw a whalebone or run outside and lay tarmac on the street.

"Will I know when it starts to happen?" he asked

"You will know," I replied. "You will definitely know."

Dessert was a variety of fritters dipped in a pink mixture of Bazooka bubble gum and melted rubber glove. I stared into the plate and tried to find a small corner of the mess that was edible. When I looked up, Chris was smiling stupidly, and then he laughed. I'd never heard him laugh before so I wasn't sure if what I heard now was the result of English public school or quality

Moroccan hash. People from other tables started looking at us. The waiters huddled in a corner and exchanged Hindi words of concern, and then Chris did it again. This time, it was pirate-from-the-Spanish-Main-meets-little-old-lady-on-a-rollercoaster. A waiter came to our table and asked if everything was okay. Perhaps we might like some tea?

"Are you expecting Zulus?" I asked.

Chis doubled over and from under the edge of the tablecloth, I heard him choke on the word "Zulus". The waiter waited for Chris to recover, but the effect was only beginning. When Chris sat upright, a change had taken place. Something dark and inexplicable was happening.

"I feel strange."

"You're meant to feel strange."

"I feel like I'm going to die."

"You're meant to feel like you're going to die."

I tried to restart the laughter, but his eyes misted over and a tear emerged. The waiter, standing awkwardly beside us all this time, looked down at me and said the worst thing he could possibly say, the worst thing imaginable. Only five words, well-intentioned and delivered in a gentle tone of voice, but devastating.

"Is your dad all right?"

Chris looked first at me and then at the waiter and then, with rising panic, at the exit.

"He's fine," I said. "He just needs some air."

Chris knocked over his chair in a sudden bolt for the door. I was so high, between the pills and the pot, I could have wiped my mouth with a ten-pound note and left four napkins as a tip.

Outside, I caught a glimpse of coat-tail disappearing around a corner. "Chris!" I called out but he didn't answer. When I caught up on him, he was clawing at the shutters of the Leicester Square tube.

"I have to get home."

"The tube isn't running."

"Your dad!" he whimpered. "Do I really look like your dad?"

I looked at Chris, with his tweeds, his boxcloth braces and his captoe Oxfords. To be honest, he looked more like my granddad.

"I thought we could be..."

I didn't let him finish the sentence. I grabbed him by the lapels and pushed him up against a shop window. It was like trying to position a mannequin with broken legs. Did I bloody well have to spell it out for him? Maybe I did. Maybe I needed to shout it in his face as loud as I could. "DON'T YOU GET IT, CHRIS? I LIKE WOMEN."

A look of bafflement spread across his face. "So do I," he said. "So do I, you bloody fool. I was about to say 'friends.' I thought we could be friends." He pushed past me and flagged down a taxi. He jumped inside and was gone.

"Oh!" I said to the emptiness of Charing Cross Road.

I turned and started to walk, with no destination in mind. I paused on High Holborn, and said "oh!" one more time. A minicab cruised up beside me and stopped. I got in and gave the address of a dealer in Walthamstow. The driver nodded and swung the cab around. He fiddled with the radio until he found some music with a heavy bass that shook the chassis.

We stopped at a traffic light beside a chip shop in Stoke Newington. Inside, a plump girl sat on a plastic chair with a brown paper bag on her lap. Above her, a sagging helix of flypaper, speckled with tiny death. She wore a white T-shirt and white pants. A roll of fat circled her waist like a ring buoy. She pulled a deep-fried saveloy from the bag and was about to take a bite when she saw me looking. Ashamed, she hid meaty log back inside the bag. I looked away. She looked away.

This is what happens when fat girls play hide the sausage.

The cab moved on through the night, skimming streets I had never seen before. I was always surprised by the size of this fucking place. Before I'd arrived, London was Big Ben, Tower Bridge and the Houses of Parliament, all squeezed together inside a snow dome. Now it was a giant red-brick bacterial colony, expanding exponentially, eating up the healthy green body of the Home Counties, killing everything it touches.

A man on a grasshopper-green Kawasaki pulled up beside us. The bike sounded like a chainsaw stuck in knotty hardwood and when he blipped the throttle, a thick vapour of engine oil coughed out from three fluted pipes. He tapped his left foot, cut down a gear and swept into the lane ahead of us. His tail bulb, shaken loose by vibration, signalled a message in bursts of three: three long flashes. I remembered from my days in the boy scouts that this was the letter "O". Oscar. Man overboard.

I thought about Chris, up to his neck, waving and looking for a ship, looking for friendship, bewildered and wrecked in the back of his taxi, the swell of London rising and falling around him. I thought about the girl in the chip shop. I thought about my mother in the ground and my girlfriend in another man's bed. I thought about the letter "O". Oscar. Man Overboard.

The cab driver caught me in the mirror, "Hey man, did you say something?"

"Yes," I replied, "I said 'Oh!'"

"Oh?" said the driver, as he turned up the radio.

19

EMPIRE

"Gosh Barry, haven't seen you in ages! Do come in, do come in."

Only in England could you have a polite drug dealer called Augustus. The dealers in Ireland are all vile little creatures with small moustaches and names that end with "o". Anto, Philo, Dommo, Scummo.

"Is that a friend of yours?" asks Augustus, pointing to the car.

"No, it's a mini-cab," I say. "He'll wait."

Augustus is upset by this extravagance. His bike with its wicker basket almost blocks the hallway. A foot soldier in the great transportational war, he rarely uses cabs, buses or tubes. He closes the door after glancing one more time at the mini-cab. "Should we ask him in?"

"No".

Like most college-educated Brits, he worries about the working man and his struggle with the forces of capital. My attitude is more fundamental: fuck 'em.

Augustus is a pale beanpole with a long, shaggy beard and a hefty dong. I know this last detail because of the picture over the mantle in the living room: Augustus and Deirdre on a shingle beach near Brighton, nude, cold and speckled with gooseflesh. Deirdre has small, uninteresting breasts and a bush the size of a tumbleweed. She waves at the camera: under her arm, more shrubbery.

I see that Augustus is holding a melodica. "I always wanted to learn an instrument," he says.

"Is the melodica an instrument?"

"Gosh, it's very difficult to master. It's like playing a small piano sideways in your mouth."

We stand in the shabby gothic hallway. A strong draft chases about our ankles and lifts the peeling wallpaper. A *Belle Époque* hat-stand rises up from the gloom like a three-headed serpent and the hiss of closed conversation comes from the other side of the living room door.

"Would you like to join us?" asks Augustus.

I say no, I'm not feeling too social. He hands me a small pill bottle and I give him £20.

"Mind if I use your bathroom?" I ask.

"My home is your home," he says. "But do you mind if I say something? You really want to be careful with that stuff."

I nod. He looks like a threadbare country doctor, and he cares. None of the dealers in Ireland – not Anto, not Philo nor Robbo – gives a damn about anybody's health. They peddle powders laced with ground-up glass and gypsum, brick dust and rat poison. They are dark chefs in hell's kitchen, forever spitting in the foul narcotic soup.

In the bathroom, I check the tablets. "OC" on one side and "10" on the other. Big guns. Bang-bang. I take two, crush them and put them under my tongue.

There is no mirror in the bathroom, just a small painting of a bridge on a sleepy river. It reminds me of the bridge at home, where young people waste time and watch each other.

One summer day, a man lost control of his motorcycle and cracked into the corner wall on the bridge. It didn't happen with any great force. In fact it hardly seemed to involve enough energy to break a bone, but it did: it broke the long bone of life. We stood around him waiting for the ambulance. No one dared move him, but somebody opened the visor on his helmet. The last thing he saw was a motley collection of denim and worn corduroy. The last thing he smelled was patchouli oil and Major cigarettes.

The ambulance appeared and a guard arrived on a bicycle. The ambulance driver opened the back doors and pulled out a stretcher whilst the guard got down on one knee and whispered an act of contrition into a cold ear. The ambulance made a pointless journey to the District Hospital, where death could not be reversed, and the guard pulled the motorcycle into the post office gateway. The back tyre dragged on the warm tarmac and a cracked sump leaked engine oil in the shape of a question mark. With death swept away, the young people went back to watching each other.

The underside of my tongue is numb and the buzz is beginning to hit. How long have I been standing at the sink? One minute? Five minutes? Ten? I pull back the brass bolt and leave the bathroom. The hall is dark, except for the bright rectangle around the living room door. I should leave, but I go towards the light.

In the living room, Deirdre holds a candle aloft. She is a high priestess in tie-dyed cheesecloth, her earrings the size of piston rings. She makes her own jewellery, with more silver than restraint. Augustus blows into the melodica and for some reason I am reminded of St. Patrick's day back home and the Presentation girls in navy pinafores. They marched behind a fat nun who pounded on a big bass drum that hung suspiciously close to her clitoris.

"Barry, so nice to see you." Deirdre kisses me on the cheek. I look around the room and recognize Edmund Walford, an old school chum of Augustus. He has a plummy accent, a wool suit and a loose black tie. Behind him, a skinny man whose name I think is Hughie sits at the dining table, looking nervous. He is Welsh or Scottish, but it doesn't matter because he never speaks. Finally, resting like a pasha on a beanbag, is a big black man with a joint in his mouth. I don't know him, but he gives me a thumbs-up, and laughs like a circus clown. His shoes are off and he wears tartan socks. I've never seen a man look more comfortable.

Deirdre puts some brown powder on a sheet of tinfoil and warms it up with the candle. The powder turns into liquefied pellets that dodge about like scared insects.

I glance at the portrait over the mantle, the chilly Augustus with his *kielbasa* unfurling and Deirdre with her tangled black alpaca. I realise something immediate and profound: nudists made my skin crawl.

Edmund Walford wags a finger in my direction as he tries to identify me. "Last time we met, you were in the company of a young lady. She was quite stunning. Irish lass. Am I right?" He presses his temples and forces out a thought. "I'm thinking of Kipling," he says. "Why am I thinking of Kipling? Has it got something to do with her name?"

"Yeah," I say, "her name is Rudyard." I do not want to talk about my ex-girlfriend.

The black dude with the tartan socks, prompted by the name

of the poet of Empire, launches into recitation in a deep booming bass:

"Take up the White Man's burden –
Send forth the best ye breed –
Go bind your sons to exile
To serve your captives' need;
To wait in heavy harness,
On fluttered folk and wild –
Your new-caught, sullen peoples,
Half-devil and half-child."

The black dude laughs and slaps the floor with the palm of his hand, sending a cascade of hash sparks into the carpet.

"Her name is Kim," says Walford, snapping his fingers. "What happened to her? Is she still around?"

I don't answer. She is gone because she is sick of me. I am also sick of me, but I'm stuck with that.

One mid-summer night I sat on that bridge, on the wall close to the weir, where I always sat. I could see her approaching. She wore a light-brown jacket and a pair of cream slacks, slip-on shoes, no socks.

"I had a dream about you last night," she said. "We were throwing snow at each other."

"Snowballs," I said.

"No, just snow."

Then she walked away.

A week later, there was a dance in the rugby club. I hated rugby and I hated dances, but most of all, I hated crap bands. Why do you need a licence for a fishing rod, but any cunt can pick up a guitar? A slow song started, and all the loaded Lotharios who were nursing their semi-erections through the protracted murder of "Jumpin' Jack Flash" hit the floor like launched torpedoes, aimed amidships at big girls who mostly looked unsinkable. I turned to leave, because it all seemed impossible and pointless – and there was Kim Sutton, looking at me looking lost, looking for her.

That was when the madness started. The courtship was fast and dangerous with unprotected sex and furious, curious fumbling in the double-seats at the Coliseum picture house, back row.

Once, we stayed out all night. The next day, her father summoned me. He sat me down in a chair deliberately placed too close to the stove. "She's sixteen years old," he said as I started to cook, "and you can keep her out any night you want, as long as you don't mind marrying her." He was a man with a cluster of good-looking daughters and he believed in a flexible, practical morality. "Do you understand what I'm saying?"

The sweat rolled down and I nodded.

He threw another shovel of coal into the stove and looked through the flames until his face lit up like a Halloween mask. "That girl gets into trouble," he said, sliding back the iron lid with a heavy poker, "you'll either be wearing a wedding suit or a shroud. Am I clear?"

I nodded again. There would be less unprotected sex in the future.

Kim Sutton laughed when she heard the details. "He does that to all the boyfriends," she said. "We call it the 'hot coals treatment.'"

Six months later, after her final exams, she hit the road, and I followed. It was all good, until it was all bad. I didn't mean to become mean, but I did.

"Hello!" says Walford with a snap of his fingers. "Anybody home? I asked you a question."

I don't like his tone. "You'll find it hard to snap those fingers when they're stuck up your fucking arse," I reply.

The room goes as quiet as the inside of a stopped clock. Augustus lets the melodica slide from his lips and Deirdre shakes her head in an effort to dislodge my rudeness. The Welsh Scot says nothing, but his eyes explore the darkest parts of the room. The big black dude blows out smoky air with a swivel of his neck, like a human oscillating fan. He alone seems unperturbed by my behaviour.

"I have to go," I say, and no one asks me to stay. Augustus brings me to the hallway where the same cool breeze dodges around our ankles.

"It's just a habit of his," he says. "Edmund. He tends to snap his fingers."

"He snapped, I snapped," I say.

Augustus frowns and becomes the country doctor once more. "I think we'll have to adjust your medication."

He really does care. He is the sweetest dealer in the world, a darling dealer, and I don't deserve him. I belong back amongst the Irish scumbags, the Mickos, the thickos and the sickos with their crushed glass and powdered laxative designed to cut holes in your nose.

I leave the house and walk down the garden path. The sky is full of sparks that look like stars. Everything wobbles. Parked outside the gate, the cab is empty, abandoned, but the meter inside is still running. I look around, expecting to see the driver relieving himself on a bush, or returning with a bag of greasy chips.

Nothing.

Off in the distance, the Post Office tower points upwards like a tottering pile of crockery. When you don't know a city, you can head in any direction and end up nowhere.

The brightness in the sky is most intense in one particular place. It's probably the West End. I start to walk. It's a good time to think about Kim Sutton. The arguments and the tears, the punctuation of slammed doors, the light brown jacket, cream slacks, slip-on shoes, no socks.

We were throwing snow at each other and now she's in fucking France.

I hear Deirdre's voice: "Take it easy, Gerald."

The black dude leaves the house and she closes the door behind him. He strolls down the garden path with the joint sizzling in his mouth. "Where you going, man?" he asks. "You know you can't leave without me."

I'm confused.

He shakes a bunch of keys and jumps into the taxicab.

I'm even more confused. "You're the driver?"

He laughs and fires up the engine. "Who did you think I was?"

I get in on the passenger side. He hands me the joint as he fiddles with the radio. A voice tells us that the new pope will soon visit Britain. "After John-Paul," I say, "what are the chances that the next pope is called George-Ringo?"

Gerald does his Barnum & Bailey laugh and takes back the joint. "You are so stoned, baby," he says. "So, so, so, so stoned."

20

WATERMARK

SATURDAY, AUGUST 25, 1979

I ran my finger down the column in the back of the *Evening News* and found a man in Ealing with a one-bed close to the tube.

"I'm looking for someone a bit more..." He didn't finish the sentence, but the word he was looking for was "English".

"I don't need much space," I said. "Just enough room to build a small bomb."

He hung up.

A man in Camden Town with a raspy voice said, "I would like a young man to share. How do you feel about sharing?"

"I don't mind doing the dishes or mopping the floor," I said, but I knew he was talking about my body.

I came to a small ad that said: CHELSEA. BASEMENT. SUIT SINGLE MAN. There was no phone number, just an address on Ifield Road.

Maura was originally from Mullingar. She wore a white blouse, a plaid skirt and she had twice as many rings as fingers. "I knew I'd catch an Irishman with that advertisement," she said. "The English won't answer anything without a telephone number at the end of it."

She made me a cup of tea and neatly arranged four biscuits around the saucer at twelve, three, six and nine. She lit a cigarette and blew the smoke sideways, towards a sealed-up fireplace. She switched off the radio and studied me.

"You're neat," she said. "You don't look like you work on the buildings."

I told her I had an office job and she raised both eyebrows.

"An Irishman with an office job!" The way she said it, it sounded absurd, like a chimpanzee with a sports car or a Martian in a bungalow.

I told her about the open-plan office in Hayes, the coffee machine, the engineers, the architects, the secretaries, and my own role as draughtsman at Calder Hall, home of Britain's military plutonium.

"They have a coffee machine?" she said, clearly impressed.

I asked her how she'd ended up in Chelsea, but she didn't explain. She just coughed out a confusion of smoke and said, "An Irishman with a clean job and an Irishwoman with a fancy house. We're quite the pair aren't we?"

I heard something rustle in the corner. Close to the window, in a high-backed armchair, a man in his early sixties sat reading the newspaper. He had a little silver question mark of hair in the middle of his head and his cheeks had been rubbed with hard soap. One hand held the folded newspaper. The other was deep in a jacket pocket, as if he were expecting a gunfight.

"That's Himself," she said.

Himself nodded and I nodded back.

"Would you like to see the basement?" asked Maura.

141

I said yes. She brought me downstairs to a neat room with two beds, a kitchenette and a small bathroom. She pulled the floor-length curtain and revealed a French window that opened into the narrow front yard. A steep metal staircase led to the street.

"You can come and go as you please," she said. "You'll also have an upstairs key, just in case you want to visit us, but you don't have to. The rent is twenty pounds."

"Will I pay you now?" I asked.

"You haven't lived here yet," she said.

For three weeks the routine was unchanging. A low-level existence, a gentle drifting through space and doorways: leave the house at seven every morning, catch a bus, sit at a desk, then reverse the sequence. I didn't read a book or a newspaper. I didn't own a radio or a television. I spoke to no one. The world was beyond reach and time was endless.

Most evenings I came back to the room and sketched in charcoal, or scribbled bad poetry on the backs of old drawings, brought home from the office. Every Saturday I put twenty pounds in an envelope and slipped it under the door upstairs. On the fourth Saturday, the door opened before I'd had time to leave.

"I never answered your question," said Maura.

"What question?"

"How did a little girl from Mullingar end up in a grand place like this?"

We sat at the round table and she filled two glasses with vodka. The football chants from Stamford Bridge rose up over Brompton cemetery, and the sing-song of hate sounded playful and sweet in the distance.

"Chelsea," Maura said. "They're playing Wrexham. Do you follow the soccer?"

I said I didn't, and she said she didn't. I thought it was a waste of time and energy and she thought it was a waste of green grass and open space. A roar went up. "Win, lose or draw," she said, "they'll break windows on the Fulham Road tonight."

Himself stirred in the shadows, a sack of tired bones lifting itself from the armchair. As awkward as it must have been, his right hand never left his pocket. "I'll go to the shop before the match is over," he said.

He crammed a hat onto his head and left the house. His shape paused outside the window and Maura remarked, "That man's a saint, a walking saint. He's always been my number-one concern. I've always looked after him. No one can say otherwise."

The shape moved on. Maura continued, "I came to London when I was very young, very young. The war was ten years over, but the place was marked. Fine streets had empty interruptions where the bombs had landed. You could see the smoke damage and the broken bricks piled on wasteland. People were still lean and hungry. They looked like they were ready to devour each other, but they didn't have the energy."

"I met Himself at a dance. He was a good dancer and he always bought nice shoes. Look at his feet when he comes back. He has fine-looking feet. We were married within the year. We started a family. We had three lovely babies, one after another, but each one died before it reached my arms. Something in my blood was killing them, and it turned out it wanted to kill me too."

"In the summer of 1959, a doctor in the Royal Marsden told me I'd be dead by Christmas. 'Go home and prepare for hardship,' he said. Hardship. He was right about that. 'And pain,' he said, 'terrible pain.' Right on both counts. But I didn't die. I came through the worst of the agony and crawled out the other side like a dog from a shipwreck, and do you know what I promised myself, my New Year's resolution for 1960? I swore I'd live every day as if it was my last."

Another roar reverberated and Maura took a sip of vodka. She wasn't a fast drinker. "That's two nil to Chelsea," she said, and winked at my surprise. "When you live here long enough, you get to know the crowd. Where was I?"

"New Year's resolution."

"Aye. Himself would come home from work and I'd have his dinner ready. I'd sit him down, give him his newspaper, turn on the radio, put a mug of sweet tea within easy reach – and then I'd hit the town. I was a bad girl and he was a saint. He saved me then and he's saving me still."

She looked towards Himself's empty chair.

"The city was alive back then, and I was dying. I stood out in a crowd. I was a wraith, a trace of a girl with black eyes, black hair and a black future. Men and women were attracted to me because tragedy always draws an audience. And there was one old man, you'd recognise his name if I said it – he was famous for being dissolute and shameful. He wanted... He wanted to hold something young and watch it die. He wanted to squeeze the spark until it became a cinder. He was so tormented with desire, he said he'd give me anything I wanted – and that's how I got this house. But of course it wasn't for me, it was for Himself. I did a deal for the deeds with the devil, but look how things worked out. The devil is gone and I'm still here. I stayed hot and he turned cold."

I finished my vodka and looked at the door.

"You think there's no more to this story," she said, "but there's more. The pain came back in 1963 and it was worse than ever before. I lasted into April and then I couldn't take it anymore. I kissed Himself on the cheek and I went to the river. I walked down the steps until the water was up to here."

She marked a line across her chest.

"I stood there and waited. What was I waiting for? I was waiting for a nudge from the water. I wasn't much of a Catholic, but I wouldn't do that. I wouldn't do it myself. I needed a hand. The hand of God. I stood there for an hour or more, the dark funnels of current dodging around me, the wash from the boats lifting me off my feet, but always dropping me back in the exact same place. The hand of God never touched me. Instead, another hand took control of my destiny. Himself. He started praying that very night and he hasn't stopped since. You've seen the hand in the pocket? That's the Rosary beads, running through his fingers like water."

She offered to refill my glass, but I said no.

She said, "Stay there for a moment. I want to show you something before you go, in case you think you've been listening to the sound of an old woman dreaming."

She went upstairs. I heard footsteps, and then wire hangers dragging on a rail. She came back down carrying a dress, the breast marked with a brown horizontal tidemark. She held it to her body and stood in the middle of the room, breathing in the smell of dark water, long since gone to the sea.

Himself returned. His fingers tumbled around inside his pocket. He sat and watched the television, and never said a word. A massive roar from Stamford Bridge shook every headstone in Brompton Cemetery, every crumbling urn and lead-lined coffin, all the leaning crosses and tilted scrolls. The gates of the mausoleum, the dome of the chapel and the keystones in the colonnades, all trembled, as did the cherubs and angels marking the plots where the babies lay.

"Three nil," said Maura.

"Aye," replied Himself. "Three, nil."

21

DOGS

Three years ago, Nicky D'Arcy was in a seminary. There are different accounts as to why he never made it to holy orders, but the one I like best is the one he dispenses himself: "I broke a blackboard over a priest's back."

"Why?"

"Because I liked the sound it made."

Everything about Nicky D'Arcy is two sizes too big. His hair is a wild mane, a rope unravelled and dipped in teak oil. The gold hoop earrings swinging from his lobes are heavier than stirrups. His shoulders are wider than doorways, and doorknobs get lost in his fist. Plus, he's crazy. It's as if someone had taken two lunatics and rolled them into one. The psychosis shines in his eyes when he swaggers on the King's Road or Oxford Street. His madness cuts a path through pedestrians, so that he never has to break his stride.

Nicky travels with an associate known as "the Madra", a

sleepy-eyed hippie who soaks up porter like a man-sized sponge. Nicky and the Madra commute regularly to Berlin, Paris and Amsterdam, yet they never appear in public bearing luggage. Their movements are secret. They sleep in the long grass or crash in a houseboat squat on the Amstel River. They are dealers of dangerous substances.

I meet them in a small pub in Fulham. Three middle-aged men, illuminated like Apollo controllers at Cape Canaveral, sit at the bar and watch television. We take our drinks to the lounge area where a video game flicks a square dot against a wall of bricks. It's like watching sperm attacking an ovum. We sit in an alcove, beneath a framed Union Jack inscribed "To Gerry the Landlord OC, from the boys of 1st Para."

The Madra keeps looking at his watch. "We have a midnight bus to catch," he says.

Nicky asks me, probably in jest, whether I would like to join them but I tell him I would prefer to sleep on a mattress stuffed with live rats, which, come to think of it, is probably what you would get in a Dutch riverboat.

The conversation, mostly conducted by the Madra, is about people back home in the Rainy Town, stragglers and misfits, pricks in the bramble bush of life "Remember Big Paul?" he asks. "He rode his bike into the river. He thought he could cycle on water. It was a Jesus thing."

"Even Jesus didn't try it on a bicycle," I reply.

The Madra drones on for a while, and then falls silent. He goes to the jukebox and lights it up with a ten-penny piece. "The House of the Rising Sun" bawls out from the big speaker behind the metal grille. "I love this song," he says.

The whine of the Vox Continental and Eric Burdon's immensely annoying squeal combine to fill the bar with an echo of falsetto regret. The Madra plays imaginary piano keys on the beer-wet table and the three men on their stools swivel as one to show disapproval. Halfway through the first wailing chorus, Gerry the Landlord comes out from behind the counter, reaches to the back of the machine and turns down the volume. Way down.

"I was listening to that," says the Madra.

"There are men here at the counter," Gerry the Landlord replies, returning to his spot behind the taps. "Men!"

I look towards the three men at the bar and realise something I should have caught before. They are all ex-soldiers, as is Gerry the Landlord.

Nicky produces a brown pill bottle from the flapped pocket of his Wrangler jacket.

"Take a free sample," he says, "and pass it back."

The bottle is old and discoloured, the name of the original patient and pharmacy scratched away. Benzedrine from the 1950s. Antique narcotics. I take two pills and swallow.

The Madra talks about a cat he owned called Fur Suit, an animal the size of a small stuffed sofa, with eyes as big as saucers. "The women cuddled him first, and then they cuddled me. I was nothing without that cat. He got me into bed with ladies who wouldn't have normally touched me."

"A pussy-magnet," I suggest.

The Madra laughs. "You're a dry bastard," he says, slapping me on the knee.

The Queen appears on the TV screen, reading a prepared speech. Her lips tremble with emotion but we pay her no attention. Then the Madra barks, "Raaaaaawruff!"

I've heard he does this sometimes, that he just can't help himself.

Gerry the Landlord bangs a glass ashtray on the counter.

"Raaaaaawruff!" goes the Madra.

Gerry the Landlord looks up at his television Queen and silently promises loyal protection. The three ex-soldiers turn on their stools and sizzle like revolving chunks of kebab meat, but they are no longer young, no longer the regimented boys from Aden and Suez. They have become nothing more than mechanisms for sucking the cancer out of untipped cigarettes. Only in their dreams will they ever fight again.

The TV cuts to wreckage on an Irish beach. A plum chap from the BBC talks about a bomb in Sligo and I hear the name Mountbatten mentioned. Cut to the Queen, a tear in her eye for the loss of her cousin.

"Raaaaaawruff!" shouts the Madra, and he almost seems embarrassed by the fact he can't stop.

Gerry the Landlord approaches, enraged.

"You three... Time to leave."

"It isn't closing time," says the Madra.

"For you, it is."

Ice forms around Nicky's eyes. He looks at Gerry the Landlord and says, "We're not going anywhere."

"You're leaving here, now."

Nicky's eyes glitter in amusement. The three old soldiers inflate themselves inside their Oxfam jackets, but all they really want is peace in our time.

"I'm going to count to three."

"Don't do that," says Nicky. "You'll just look foolish when we're still here."

"Think you're funny, do you mate?"

Nicky doesn't move. I remember seeing him in a fight, back in Ireland. It was like watching a ballet where people got hurt.

"Right," says Gerry the Landlord. "Get out of here, NOW!"

The Madra looks nervous, but Nicky puts his hands behind

his head, like a man preparing for slumber. To reinforce the image, he leans back and closes his eyes.

Gerry the Landlord goes to a door on the closed-in staircase, bangs it with his fist and in the upstairs distance something stirs. Not something human. Something claw-footed and heavy-boned. It moves quickly over linoleum flooring and, when it reaches the stairs, comes tumbling down like a careless delivery of lumber. It hurls itself against the door, scratching and yelping. Gerry the Landlord turns to us. A lusty beam of victory lights up his face.

"You want a dog? I'll give you a dog."

The claws rip at the woodwork, pulling nails and knots from the planking.

The Queen puts down her prepared speech, crumples it into a ball and tosses it over her shoulder. This may be another one of those dire moments, when British firepower triumphs over the pure guts of a lesser nation. This might be the battles of Crécy, Blenheim and Waterloo, rolled into one.

Nicky opens his eyes and something dangerous awakens, something deadly, instantly recognised by the old soldiers. The dog barking intensifies. Gerry the Landlord puts his hand on the brass knob and starts to twist. The howling grows louder.

"Will you leave, or must we let out the dog?" purrs the Queen.

Nicky stands, slowly, and Gerry the Landlord is surprised by the height, width and sheer muscle of this Pat, this Psycho-Pat. His hand trembles on the knob as he turns it another few degrees.

Nicky reaches down, plucks the three-legged stool from the floor and holds it up by one leg. He looks straight through Gerry and into the Queen's watery eyes and says,

"Let out the fucking dog."

Suddenly I love this giant of a man.

"LET-OUT-THE-FUCKING-DOG!"

At a stroke, 800 years of calamitous and humiliating defeats are wiped from the slate of history. It does not matter what happened under Cromwell's whip or Cornwallis's hoof. This is a victory of historic proportion. In Selma, Alabama, it was "We shall overcome"; for the French it was "*Liberté, egalité, fraternité*"; for the Cubans, "*La lucha continua*"; and for the Israelis, "*Kadima!*" Finally, the Irish have their own battle cry, an instantly recognizable call to arms.

"LET OUT THE FUCKING DOG!"

Gerry the Landlord drops his hand from the doorknob, and the three old military kit-bags turn away, back towards the carnage on the television. The Queen looks vanquished; not even God can save her. We hold our ground. Nicky passes around the pack of Drum tobacco and we all roll up and luxuriate in the thick smoke of the battlefield. We relax and let the clock tick away until closing time. Then, on the stroke of eleven, we stand. We march toward the exit with heads held high. We pause at the jukebox, and Nicky inserts another ten-penny piece. He reaches behind the machine and turns up the volume. Way up.

The air outside is warm and muggy. I pocket the pill bottle and slip a ten-pound note into Nicky's massive hand. The darkness separates us. A bus is waiting somewhere to take them through listless hours and heaving sea, into the heart of a foreign land. I should go with them. I should, but something keeps me rooted here, in this moment, in this city, in this England.

22

BURNING

Kevin had bought a Nikon camera from two kids who were running past his bus stop. "They were thieves," he said, as if the matter needed clarification. "I asked them where they got it, and they said Fleet Street."

"That's great," I said. "Now you know where to find the owner."

He twiddled with the f-stops and rolled the focus back and forth. "It's probably professional gear," he said, catching me in the viewfinder. He was excited.

"Please don't take a picture of me on a stolen camera."

"No film in it," he said. "I think I'll go with Kodachrome. Slides. I bought a projector a few months ago.

"Same bus stop?" I asked.

He ignored me. "I have an idea for some really good snaps."

Kevin was a compulsive collector and trader. He was at his happiest strolling through a market on a Saturday morning, examining the junk and riling the stallholders.

"I'll give you two quid for it."

"If you looked at the label, you would see the price is seven pounds."

"C'mon, you won't get seven pounds for that gadget."

The angry stall-holder would turn their attention to another customer, if there was another customer, but that wouldn't stop Kevin.

"I'll give you two-fifty. Final offer."

"The item is not for sale for two-pounds fifty."

"You'll be taking it home and bringing it out again next Saturday. All that hauling around... it's hard on your back."

"Thank you for considering my health, but I don't think we will be doing business."

"Three quid. Take it or leave it. I couldn't go another penny."

"Could you please move along?"

"You drive a hard bargain. Three twenty-five and you don't need to wrap it."

"I'll call the market manager."

"Three pounds thirty. You're breaking my heart here."

"This is the last time I'll say this, the price is seven pounds."

"Three forty-five."

"No!!"

At this point, Kevin would grin and pat the stall owner on the shoulder before he walked away. "I'll see you next week."

He always offered less than half the asking price. Sometimes a lot less. "What would you call an offer like that?" he once asked me.

"Derisory," I said.

"Derisory," he repeated. Kevin loved new words. He collected them the way he collected stolen goods. He'd left school at fifteen years of age and moved to London. I was his dictionary. His curiosity towered above him. He needed to know things.

He needed to know everything. I had given him "obfuscate" and "oblique". He used them sparingly: he worked on the building sites, and big words could get a man in trouble.

Once, at the Earl's Court Motor Show, he'd opened a car door stealthily, like a hoodlum, looking left and right, before sitting in. "*Covetous*, and maybe a little *acquisitive*," he'd said.

We had been apart for three years while I finished my education. Kevin only came back to Ireland once in that time, for his father's funeral.

"Come on," he said as we left the cemetery. "Let's go for a drive."

He'd brought back a Triumph Stag on the ferry, all British racing green, cream leather seats and burl walnut dashboard. He was just about old enough to have a licence, but he didn't bother. The car sounded furious when he revved it, and he revved it a lot. We took off on a long racing loop that brought us through Tramore, Rosslare and Courtown. Seaside towns filled with hustle and noise. Kevin went into at least ten different shops that day, busy little waterfront places with racks of flip-flops and colourful kites hanging from the ceilings. In one shop he bought two buckets, two spades and a beach towel with seagulls on it. In another, four hula-hoops and a couple of ice creams. We both ended up wearing kiss-me-quick bowlers and cheap plastic sunglasses. In each shop, he paid with a twenty-pound note. I thought he was showing off, letting me see how well he was doing in England. We smoked a joint on the beach at Ballymoney and watched the evening sun hop off the rusty shipwreck. We took some pills he'd brought over, but they just made us awkward and unbalanced, like ice skaters who suddenly found themselves wearing snowshoes.

"If I knew what these things were," said Kevin, tossing the

little brown bottle into the brine, "I'd never buy them again."

He told me about London. "You better get over there quick," he said. "Don't wait until the 1980s."

"Why not?"

"It'll all be over."

"What?"

"You won't know if you don't come."

We drove back to the Rainy Town via Gorey, Ferns and Bunclody. He stopped and bought a road map in a petrol station, with another twenty-pound note, but as soon as we got back on the road, he tossed it out the window.

"Is that supposed to be symbolic?" I asked.

"Yeah, something like that."

I asked him if he had one word to describe his father, what would it be. He thought about it for a while.

"Inscrutable. I never knew anything about him. He kept himself to himself, didn't say much. He could love you or he could hate you, and you'd never know which."

It actually sounded as if he was describing himself.

"He once gave me two shillings for watching the gate."

"Watching the gate?"

"Yeah. He was heading out the door and he said, 'I want you to keep an eye on that gate until I get home.' So, I stood there watching the gate. Everybody saw me. The postman. The milkman. Anyone on the street. Some of them asked what I was doing and I told them. They thought I was cracked. He was gone for half the day and when he came back, he'd had a few drinks. He says, 'Did you watch that gate?' I said I did. 'Did you take your eye off it?' 'Not once.' 'Are you sure?' 'I'm dead sure.' He gave me two shillings."

"Why do you think he did that?"

"I think he wanted to give me the money, but he didn't want to give it to me for nothing."

Before we got home, we made one more stop. The dolmen on the hill overlooking the Rainy Town, a 5,000-year-old tomb made from standing blocks of granite, with a capstone the size of a bus. We climbed atop and smoked one last joint.

"They say there's a chieftain buried underneath this thing," he said. "I wonder if he took anything valuable with him."

"Well, we do have two little shovels in the back of the car."

"He must have been important for them to build something like this."

The clouds turned black, as the rain got ready to fall.

"I need to get a headstone for the father," he said.

"They'll notice if this thing goes missing."

He laughed for the first time that day. We both laughed. It was decent dope.

The next day he was gone, and it was some time later that I discovered the reason for the hula-hoops, the buckets and spades, the kiss-me-quick hats and the map that went out the window. The twenty-pound notes were forged and had to be got rid of as quickly as possible. I was disappointed he hadn't told me. I might have been excited, if I'd known we were breaking the law.

The rain hammered nails into roof tiles and London squelched under the deluge. In my room, I fed broken coat-hangers into a flickering fire and imagined the punishment of hell.

The devil's greatest weapon is fire. A thousand years ago, that might have been a big deal, but these days any prick with a Bic can burn down a house. He created flame, but we'd come right back at him with asbestos.

Did I mention I was stoned?

Extremely stoned.

Devilishly stoned.

Downstairs, somebody rang the bell, but nobody answered. That's how it goes when you live in flats. Silence and withdrawal is an anti-bailiff strategy. I ignored it too, until it became apparent that some lunatic was kicking down the door. Then I knew it was for me.

Kevin stood on the front step, shielding a slide projector with a tartan umbrella. "I've got something to show you," he said.

In my room, he loaded four slides into the carousel. "Turn off the light," he said, sniffing the air. "Were you smoking opium in here?"

"No," I lied.

"You look pale," said Kevin.

"It's a fashionable look. What exactly are you doing?"

"I told you I had an idea for some snaps." He adjusted the lens and wiped the raindrops with the corner of his sleeve. "You can never talk about this," he said. "Nobody has ever taken pictures like this before, not in the entire history of fucking photography."

A tingle ran up my spine.

"I could end up in Pentonville, getting ridden by the ghost of Oscar Wilde."

"Not to mention Roger Casement."

Kevin swore me to secrecy as the room filled up with brimstone.

The first snap showed a bedroom illuminated by moonlight. Two nightstands; a pile of laundry in a corner; a middle-aged couple in a bed with the covers dragged down. His cheeks were puffy and pocked-marked. Her shoulders were bony, the strap on her slip held in place with a safety pin.

"Do you see the safety pin?"

"Yeah," I said.

The room looked like it was underwater, the inhabitants drowned in a quiet tragedy. The pain on their faces was old. Antique. Maybe inherited. Her fingertips touched his back. She was pushing him away in a dream, but he was as heavy as a sack of stones.

The carousel turned, and the second slide clicked into place. A living-room choked with cheap furniture, empty bottles on the floor and a saucer filled above the rim with dead cigarette butts. An old man, fully dressed, curled up asleep on a sofa, his arms folded inside an imaginary strait jacket. His mouth had been robbed of teeth and his head bumped once too often on hard objects, possibly fists. He looked like nothing good had ever happened to him. No one had ever touched or straddled him. I heard Kevin whisper, "Sad bastard."

Another slide, another bedroom: a ruin of a room, stripped plaster revealing the riven oak lath, like the ribcage of a monstrous beast. A mattress on the floor. A young couple facing each other the way young people do, their unconscious senses watching each other. They both had short hair and it was impossible to decipher their sex. Two boys? Two girls? Girl / boy? A pair of aliens with nothing between their legs but space? They were as still and symmetric as bookends.

"I don't know what they are," said Kevin, "but they're beautiful."

The carousel clicked again, revealing the starkest room of them all.

"I saved the best for last," said Kevin.

Bare wooden boards on the floor. A pair of towering windows that looked out onto a perfect blackness. A *prie-dieu*. A bedside table. A crucifix on the wall. Lying in the bed was a young woman, eyes closed, arms outside the blankets and her wrists tied together with something I couldn't quite make out.

"It's a rosary beads," said Kevin. "It's to keep her pure in the night."

She reminded me of my first girlfriend, the Sexual Ventriloquist. Her family had sent her from a bog village to learn mathematics, good manners and hair brushing techniques in the Mercy boarding school. At weekends I climbed the convent wall to meet her. We faded into the tree line around the hockey pitch and sucked each other's lips like leeches stuck to a mirror. Our mouths were connected, yet every time I tried to insert a hand into the folds of her clothing, a voice appeared from nowhere.

"That's far enough."

I still don't know how she did it. It was quite a gift.

"Are you sure you're not stoned?" Kevin asked.

I was incredibly stoned.

"Of course I'm not stoned."

"Because I need your complete understanding. I need to know that you know."

"Never mind me," I said. "What about you?"

"I'm not stoned," he snapped.

He was definitely stoned.

"Do you know the truth?" he asked.

"The truth is what you tell when nobody is listening."

Kevin nodded as if I was making sense. He turned off the projector and turned on the light. We became eerily human.

"Will you take more snaps?" I asked.

He shook his head. "The camera's already sold."

Without another word, he plucked the slides from the carousel and tossed them into the fire. The emulsion flashed and ignited. The devil himself couldn't understand these Paddies. Nothing they did made sense. He didn't want them in hell: they'd fuck the place up, the same as they did with Kilburn.

I looked at Kevin and he seemed far away. The truth was simple. He had broken into four houses, including a house of god, to steal just one thing. An image. A moment. His victims had slept through the theft and nobody would ever know, just the two of us. And the devil. This was his exhibition, and my room his gallery. Fifteen seconds of fame, followed by fifteen seconds of flame. The slides gave a last blue flash before they puffed into powder.

"Clandestine," he said.

"Arcane," I replied.

We basked in the brief warmth of his misdemeanour.

"Arcane," he said, and I could tell he liked that word. It was already added to his collection.

23

PATRIARCH

WEDNESDAY, SEPTEMBER 5, 1979

We stop at Sainsbury's to purchase a chicken. Kevin eventually finds a bird that suits his needs. "I'm happy with this chicken," he says, as though he plans on proposing marriage.

We walk up Bruce Grove smoking a spliff, and everything around us is badly lit, poorly directed and way under-budget. An Asian boy of fifteen or sixteen stops in front of us and says, "Any chance, mate?" Kevin hands him the spliff and we watch him inhale. For some reason, Kevin has a huge affection for kids who pretend they're tough.

"Cheers, mate." The Asian boy swaggers off, snapping his fingers. He probably thinks we're Brits. Kevin wears a blue blazer and a white T-shirt. I'm wearing patent leather shoes. We're going to Kevin's house for dinner.

"I've invited the Wheel," he says.

"The Wheel," aka Robbie Ferris, is a mutual acquaintance, a young man with rolling black curls and the pouty lips of a Roman senator. He hails from one of those border counties where the land is so poor, murder is the only profitable occupation.

"What time does the wheel roll into town?" I ask, but Kevin ignores the pun.

Kevin stands in the little glass lean-to at the rear of his house, assembling a P57 Mustang fighter. He's been putting together models since he was six or seven years old and when he's finished, after the last water transfer and the final dab of camouflage paint, he'll find a child and give it away. In the place where he brings his laundry, they know him as the Airplane Man.

In the kitchen, Sharon follows Kevin's baking Instructions. He has given her a menu for the night, a bunch of crumpled pages ripped from a public library cookbook. She is a year younger than Kevin, about nineteen, born and raised in West London. She has a kind smile and a warm nature, but it's anybody's guess how she got mixed up with the Irish. When Paddies and Brits end up together, it's usually the result of a hostage situation.

Sharon is the one who enforces the household rules, most of which concern narcotics. We are permitted to smoke ganja at will, but not until little Lizzy is tucked away in bed are we allowed to pop pills, chop powder, chase dragons and put sundry stuff up our noses. Most important, there will never be a needle on the premises.

Kevin's niece Catrìona is flirting, an art she has recently discovered in *Diana* magazine. She flirts with everyone and everything. She brushes past the kitchen table, touching it with her hip, and then smiles under lowered lashes. Fourteen years old and she's wearing a pair of leatherette jeans that could easily get her into trouble. She flirts with Sharon, who is too busy trying to make sense of the cooking instructions to notice. She moves on and flirts with baby Lizzy, and then she flirts with yours truly. She does this by rolling me a joint. She runs her tongue down the seam on an Embassy Regal and the blonde tobacco spills out. She takes the block of Zero-Zero from the copper kettle and cooks it over a Zippo. She crumbles, blends, rolls and twists, and then holds out the product with pride. She has discovered a great truth: the quickest way to a man's heart is through his lungs.

Little Lizzie pushes a beach ball across the floor. I lie back on the sofa and she bumps into my knees. "Oops!" she says.

"Oops!" I reply.

Kevin takes the joint and pops it into his mouth. He spins the propeller on the P-57. Lizzy runs towards him, he picks her up and says, "Oops!"

"Oops!" she replies.

The doorbell rings. The Wheel has arrived. He kisses Sharon on the cheek and slaps me on the back. Sharon likes it; I don't. I see something in his eye, and it's obvious he's high. Energized and attentive but without the gurning and the grinding, so it can't be straight speed. Drinamyl? Tuinal? He sits on the end of the sofa and starts to riff. His charm rolls out like a red carpet and the words spill down along it in one unbroken, effortless line. He is hot and cool, all at the same time. He is close to God and it is through his lips that God speaks with absolute clarity and unquestionable authority.

The bastard is doing coke!

Sharon, having found something in the recipe that alarms her, says, "Kevin, what exactly is a courgette?"

"Leave it out."

"Do you mean 'leave it out' as in 'leave-it-out, mate,' or do you want me to leave it out of the recipe?"

"Use cucumber instead."

She shakes her head and goes back to the cooker. Kevin slides back the tiny Perspex canopy and installs the pilot with a blob of glue on the seat of his pants.

I find myself thinking about Peru and massive mounds of white powder. I imagine a *campesino* with a great sack of narcotics slung over his shoulder: "*Senor*, I bring you *El Blanco Magnifico*."

El Blanco Magnifico is health food for the nasal passages, pure and untouched. It's like a virgin bride, whereas the stuff we usually snort is more like the town bike.

Sharon picks up baby Lizzy, who instantly turns into a screaming ball of mayhem and murder. She kicks and spins, but Sharon takes her firmly in her arms and promises to read a story.

"Goldilocks and the Three Bears. Porridge."

The screaming continues all the way down the hall. It stops for a moment, then starts up again. In the distance, it sounds more animal than human.

Kevin goes to the stove and pulls open the door. He prods the gratin, lifting the crust's edge with the tip of a knife. "This needs another ten minutes." He puts on an oven mitt and raises the dish to a higher level.

Catriona is full of wild energy. She stands on her tip-toes and, like a ballerina, stretches her arms high above her head. Her T-shirt pops out from her waistband and her belly button flickers for a moment. She pirouettes in front of the window and then looks out at London, or at least at the dull backside of the opposing terrace. The Wheel's upper lip shines with a speckle of perspiration as he winks discreetly in her direction. I look back to see Kevin's reaction, but he's kneeling down, staring into the open gas oven like a man considering suicide. We don't exist in his world.

Something happened, but nothing happened. Catrìona has a face filled with curiosity, which she tries to cover with an awkward smile. For an instant, I think of Kim Sutton. I see her walking on the Champs Élysées. I wonder if she still looks good, but of course she does. She had her boyfriend amputated, not her head. She disappears into a café and sits at a table with Sartre. She loves Sartre. She orders an *apéritif*. Sartre lights her Gauloise and uses his good eye to peep down the front of her blouse. Her expression is far away and lost. "If you are lonely when you are alone," says Sartre, "you are in bad company."

He doesn't see my fist coming.

Catrìona's summer in London has been nothing to write home about. She helps look after the baby, but she hasn't seen anything or gone anywhere. Once, Sharon brought her to Camden Lock market; that's where she bought those jeans. Another time she chatted with the two West Indian boys from next door, but Kevin soon put a stop to that.

"Why?" she stamped. "You wouldn't mind me talking to them if they were girls."

Kevin looked at her steadily. "Girls can't get you pregnant," he said.

She filled up with a boiling rage that condensed into a stream of tears. In a week's time, she will sail back to the Rainy Town. When her friends ask about London, she will flash a hapless smile, shrug and look away. She will be pregnant at nineteen and married at twenty and she will never go anywhere again.

I can see veins on the side of the Wheel's head, ropes branching into smaller cords, and he has a tight, tetanus cramp in his jaw. Catrìona chases after the beach ball, dropping to her knees in front of us, crawling after it. The Wheel looks down, only for an instant, at Catrìona's perfect bottom, wrapped in warm leatherette. He readjusts his focus and slightly shifts the trajectory of his attention, pretending that his eyes did not connect, but it's too late. I've seen the hunger and the savagery.

Catrìona uses her teeth to pull out the recessed valve and the beach ball deflates beneath her like a satisfied lover. The Wheel is ready to explode. I look back at Kevin, but he is just closing the oven door.

Something happened, but nothing happened.

The Wheel excuses himself and heads for the WC. Kevin turns around, looks at me and taps the side of his nose. I nod. It's bad form. If you're not going to share your gear, better to leave it at home. Don't rub people's noses in it, if you're not prepared to rub their noses in it.

Kevin goes to the stereo and selects an album from the rack: *Troubadour* by JJ Cale. I know what's coming next, and I'm excited. What can I say? Good-looking people are notoriously heartless.

We wait for the mock-flush to come from the toilet and as soon as it does, Kevin lowers the needle onto the last track, side one. He turns up the volume.

The Wheel appears. The music starts.

"I love this song," Catrìona says as she swings her hips to the twangy intro of "Cocaine".

The Wheel stops in his tracks. He's so high, he may not get the pointed message delivered in the lyrics. He looks at Kevin, he looks at me, but mostly he looks at Catrìona. Irish people, when they dance, usually resemble barefoot stroke victims hopping about on a floor covered with thumbtacks, but not Catrìona. She knows how to move.

"Robbie," she asks, "do you wanna dance?"

The Wheel doesn't need a second invitation. He interlocks his hairy hands with her delicate fingers and she laughs. They move about with a foot of daylight between them. Around and around the Wheel spins, and Catrìona finds herself trapped like a small bird in the stare of a stoat. She should pull back and yet she closes the gap between them. It's as if she has taken this moment, right here, right now, to declare her emerging womanhood.

With a movement that is both swift and incredibly agile, The Wheel slides his knee between her legs and then runs his heavy paws down her back and over the bump of her bottom.

I don't need to look around to see the lava streaming out of Kevin's eyes. Catrìona pushes the Wheel away and opens up the space between them again. Her face is red and worried. The step she took was a step too far. The Wheel rolls his lower lip into his mouth and bites down. He wants something that he can never have. The music, and time itself, scratch to a sudden stop.

Kevin strides past me with the cooked chicken in his fist. He nods at the Wheel. An invisible signal. A secret message delivered. Both men walk out through the lean-to and into the yard. Kevin tosses the chicken into the bin.

Dinner is off.

The two men face each other, but all we can see is the Wheel's ashen expression and the back of Kevin's head. Kevin talks in a silent voice and the whole thing lasts no more than twenty seconds. Kevin turns, walks back into the house, picks up the P57 Mustang, and blows some imaginary dust off the wings. He sets the plane on a small plastic tripod.

Nothing happened, but something happened.

The Wheel returns, but he doesn't even look at Catrìona. He picks up his shoulder-bag, walks to the door and exits. Catrìona's embarrassment turns into anger. This is just one more thing, one more example of Kevin's control, one more pull on the puppet string. She wants to scream, stamp her feet and slap his face. She storms up behind him, ready to pummel his back, but he senses her approach. He turns and he says one word. His voice is gentle and it stops her on the spot. He doesn't need to tell her that she is his ward and this is an ugly fucking world. He doesn't make a fuss about the leatherette jeans, the dancing, the belly button and the beach ball. He says one word, one word we have all obeyed, a word that tells us we have a place. A safe place. A place where no one can hurt us. One word.

"Bedtime."

24

SMOKE

Chris Longley no longer talks to me at work. He walks right past me as if I don't exist. A couple of times I've brought him coffee from the machine, but he lets it go cold on his desk. I have a new friend called Don. We share the same bad habits.

At lunchtime, I leave the drawing office with Don and we sit in his car on the Uxbridge Road. We smoke up a couple of blazing joints and talk the inevitable nonsense. Don is a squatter. He lives in an abandoned hospital with a wife and three children.

"We have our own ward," he said. "It's named after Alexander Fleming. Come over and check it out."

"What are the visiting hours?" I asked.

He thought that was funny.

The car, a Mark III Zephyr, fills up quickly with heavy fumes, as we play a game of "Flying Fuchs". The Flying Fuchs are an imaginary Austro-Hungarian family of trapeze artists and the game goes something like this:

Don will say, "Name the flyer that left for health reasons."

I will reply, "The sick Fuch."

"The flyer that lost his voice?" The dumb Fuch.

"The flyer that ran off and found religion?" Holy Fuch.

"The flyer with the eating disorder?" Fat Fuch.

And so on. When you're stoned it's positively hilarious.

We go back to the drawing office at half past one and Don's desk is gone. Not moved, gone, and the space closed up as if he had never been there at all. Don is totally out of it. He keeps saying, "This is peculiar," and "How am I supposed to respond to this?"

He asks me to have a word with the chief engineer.

"Don't worry," I say. "I'll get things sorted out".

Alan Mack has a boxy office, heated to extravagant temperatures by a giant cast-iron radiator. He leaves sweaty prints on everything he touches. Nobody ever shakes his hand.

"What happened to Don's desk?" I ask.

"Bad show. Heave-ho."

He actually talks like that.

"Did he do something wrong?"

Alan touches his nose with an index finger. "The hush-hush boys were here," he says, referring to Security.

"And they took Don's desk?"

"Silly sod, buggered himself."

Alan closes the door to his office and explains. Apparently, Don attended some anti-nuke rallies, and this is very bad form, especially when you work in the nuke industry.

"Peace chappies have gone to war with us," says Alan.

"Is there no way he can come back?"

Alan shakes his head.

"I thought the English always gave a man a second chance."

"No," he replies sadly. "That's the Americans. Now follow me, old bean."

I follow Alan down through the busy drawing-office and into the lift. We go up to the fourth floor and into the model room. The entire Windscale/Sellafield complex, miniaturized and made from pale blue cardboard and Foamex, sprawls out before us on twenty-five hundred square feet of pristine white linoleum. Like a fat, sweaty Gulliver, Alan carefully steps over the buildings. He takes a two-metre pointing stick from a hook on the wall and plants himself firmly in the middle of the Irish Sea. He waves the stick over Cumbria like some deranged magician, then points it at the golf ball dome that shields the UK's top atomic secrets.

"I'm giving *you* the conveyor system in the AGR, boy."

"Excuse me?"

"This is promotion, old bean. Promotion!"

"Isn't that Don's area?" I ask.

"More buttons, too."

"Buttons?"

"What's the Gaelic for money?"

"*Airgead*," I reply.

"Arry-gid. I like the sound of that. You'll be getting more arry-gid."

"How much more?" I sense I'm not doing a great job of defending Don's interests.

"I should say an extra one pound fifty per hour, old boy."

With the tip of his stick, Alan lifts the cardboard dome and exposes the Advanced Gas Cooled Reactor. He reveals an aluminium ball wrapped with tiny red and blue pipes.

"You'll be handling the spent fuel rods. Uranium dioxide, as black as your Irish heart. You know what that gives you, old bean?"

"What?"

"More fucking power than the PM. Use it wisely."

Under the hard fluorescent lighting, his laughing face looks distorted and deviant. He pulls the miniature reactor out on the tip of his stick and tosses it across the room in my direction.

I catch the reactor and fire it back. Alan swings the stick and smacks it into the Firth of Forth.

"Howzat!" he roars in pure delight, and he is no longer a middle-aged man in a ratty cardigan. He is an excited schoolboy *cocking a snook* at St Peter's of York.

Alan's father owned a small shirt factory, somewhere up north, and it had taken years of careful saving to send him to Cambridge, an ill-fitting world of books and buggery whence he had descended into the well-dug grave of civil engineering. He was angry at everything, but he hid it beneath a smile.

"What was your college in Ireland like?" he asks.

When I explain that it was a small, concrete institution where car mechanics and bookkeepers learned how to wield wrenches and sharpen pencils, he seems envious. I have nothing to live up to.

He hangs the two-metre stick on the wall and says, "You'll speak to Don. Tell him he's not coming back."

The suggestion comes out of nowhere and I am surprised.

"Don considers me a friend," I say.

"Rotten show, I know, but somebody has to stick his finger up the budgie's arse."

He plods off through the Lake District and then stomps over the Yorkshire Dales on his way to the exit. I'm speechless. Alan winks at me as he departs. "Think of the arry-gid, me boy," he says. "Think of the arry-gid."

Don is sitting in his car on the Uxbridge Road, staring fixedly out the window at a woman in a sari who is slapping a child on the legs. I get into the passenger seat and he immediately asks me about the "situation".

"I tried my best," I say. "Cutbacks, you know."

With unexpected violence and absolutely no warning he slams his head against the steering wheel. The horn beeps and the woman in the sari drags her child to safety, where she can beat him some more. "My wife is a darling," says Don. "This is going to break her heart. What do I do? I'm 32 years old."

"You still have a little time left," I say.

We both laugh, but it's a flat sort of laughter, the kind you hear at a funeral, or coming from a bank manager's office. Don pulls a joint from the glove compartment. "Smoke?"

I shake my head and say no, I have a job to get back to. I don't tell him that it's his.

"Maybe I should come with you and have a little chat with Alan Mack. If I told him about my situation…"

"Not a good idea," I say, perhaps a little too hastily.

Don squints at me, as if he senses something amiss. He lights the joint and sucks back the smoke. His mind is evidently spinning.

If it were really a case of cutbacks, why would they keep me and dispose of him? With his striped socks and frayed lapels peppered with dandruff, he is not a pretty sight, but he's a better draughtsman than I will ever be, and he knows it.

"Let's play one last game of Flying Fuchs," he says.

"I really have to get back to the office," I protest.

"Come on, for old times' sake."

It seems mean to deny him this one little thing.

"Okay," I say. "Shoot."

"What was the name of the flyer that fell and couldn't get up?" Don stares into my eyes with the beginning of a smirk on his lips.

"I have no idea," I say.

"It's a good 'un," he says. "Think about it."

We say goodbye. I head back towards the office. The rickety Zephyr engine starts up behind me and a tyre screeches against a kerbstone.

"The flyer that fell and couldn't get up?" I say aloud.

I look back and the Zephyr is gone. The woman in the sari and the child are gone. The wind twists some crisp bags up into the air outside the Hamborough Tavern. A small group of children in grey school uniforms walk over the canal bridge laughing at each other, tossing a plastic bag filled with oranges, back and forth between them. When it lands in the gutter, they walk away, pretending it isn't theirs.

I cross the bridge with quickened step, but pause for a moment and look at the bag of oranges. Something flickers: the image of a fallen man in a persimmon tunic, prostrate and motionless in the middle of a sawdust ring. Up above, an empty trapeze swings back and forth. The other Flying Fuchs gather on the wires, looking down at their fatally wounded companion. The penny drops. It all makes sense in an instant.

It is I.

I am the man who has lost lost his grip and tumbled to his doom. I am the man sprawled in the dirt, a trickle of blood trailing from my lips. I am the flyer that fell and couldn't get up.

I am the Lying Fuch.

25

INTERVIEW

SUNDAY, OCTOBER 14, 1979

"What sort of music are you into?" asks Eamon.

I am sitting in front of a panel of hippies, and the experience is unnerving. The tablecloth is a sheet of polythene that sticks to my elbows. Everything in this kitchen came from a skip and, judging by their appearance, that includes the hippies.

Siobhan is a pale and pimpled 22-year-old from some bollicky Ulster county where Mammy bakes brown bread and Daddy bleaches diesel. Every Irish squat in London has a Siobhan. "We have to ask these questions," she says, hoisting a pair of shapeless breasts over her folded arms. She looks like a balloonist getting ready to drop ballast.

Miriam is in her mid-thirties, I smile at her but she doesn't respond. There's a blockage in her expression caused by the bitter cherry of methadone. She scratches the back of her hand, the way they do.

Eamon is a Dubliner in a top hat. He's aiming for Marc Bolan meets cool, but he's coming off Abraham Lincoln meets cunt. "We're very particular about what goes on the system," he says, nodding towards the block of stereo equipment in the corner. "We had a fella in here and he polluted the air with his sounds."

"He brought a real bad vibe with him," moans Siobhan.

Norman has a dreadlocked beard, like clods of dirt hanging from his chin. He stands at the stove and opens the cupboard, revealing a ten-pound bag of lentils. He takes two spoons of tea from a Cow & Gate tin and shakes them into a dirty pot.

"We don't believe in tea bags, man."

Of course you fucking don't, *man*. Plus soap is bad for the skin and deodorant causes cancer.

"Music?" I muse. "What sort of music am I into?"

I know I can't mention hardcore punk rock. The correct answer, my gut tells me, is Bob Dylan, but that's a dangerous road to go down. Suppose they quiz me. Mr Zimmerman has at least five hundred records and I only know two of them. Hendrix? Too strident for the women. Baez? Too menstrual for the men. How about Jethro Tull?

Focus. I have to pass this test. I really need a new place to live.

This hippie house is right next door to the Imperial War Museum, where people bring their children to see how many guns it took to kill a pygmy, how much opium to enslave a nation. If the Irish had a war museum, we'd fill it with a fine collection of nail bombs and rebel songs. There would be no official closing time, just a five-minute warning to vacate the premises.

What music am I into? Think. Fast.

The curious, moonish faces all turn in my direction and await the correct reply.

I remember the first hippie I ever saw. I was nine years old in the back of a Christian Brothers classroom on the Station Road. The world beyond the frosted glass was a shapeless mess, but on this particular day, Brother Tyrell lifted the sash and the rusty weights rumbled inside the casings.

"Nobody is to look out this window," he said, "the purpose of an open window is to let the *air* in, not the *stare* out." He returned to the front of the class and scribbled something about Jesus fighting and dying for Ireland. Education was simple back then: it didn't have to make any sense at all. He underlined a sentence and then stabbed it with chalky punctuation. He circled it and stabbed it again. He roared at the blackboard and speckled it with spit.

A movement outside caught my attention. It was a young man with long black hair, bouncing along with a guitar slung over his shoulder. I could hear the train coming. The young man quickened his step. He was on his way to Dublin with a plectrum in his pocket and a song in his heart.

The train blew its long, lonesome whistle, masking the sound of Brother Tyrell as he sneaked up behind me. The big steel wheels screeched on the track and I never saw the punch coming. It knocked me sideways, clear out of the seat, onto the floor where the pain and the shock had time to awaken. The window slammed shut.

Brother Tyrell returned to the blackboard and wrote one word in yellow capital letters: AMADÁN. Fool. The class laughed because it had to. "AMADÁN!" he bellowed, and the foamy bubbles burst from his mouth until he looked like a drowning man. "What are you?"

"An amadán, brother."

"Say it again."

"An amadán, brother."

The train pulled in and I lifted myself from the floor. I looked at the man in the black frock and I said to myself, *Some day I'll watch your breed wither and die in the dirt of history. I'll go to England and join the people you despise, the people who killed God and Padraig Pearse. I'll talk their tongue and I'll live a life you can barely imagine, full of sex, sin and soccer on Saturdays. I will wipe out this memory, the same way you wipe that chalk from the board at the end of each and every day.*

Or something like that.

The hippies await their answer. I desperately need a new place to live. *Think.* I blink for a moment and in that flash of darkness, a name pops up, a perfect fit for the moment. I toss it out and hope for the best. "Neil Young," I say. "I like Neil Young."

Every face at the table smiles. Bingo. Nail on the head.

"Neil is cool," says Eamon, because he is on first-name terms with the Canadian whiner.

"What's his best album?" asks Norman.

The obvious answer is a toss-up between *Harvest* or *After The Gold Rush*, but I decide to play the goal from a different angle. I dodge and weave and tackle them from behind. "*On the Beach*," I say.

The hippies intake all the air in the room, and then let it out slowly.

"*On the Beach*?" says Eamon.

"Pretty depressing album," adds Norman.

"It's about truth," I somehow reply without laughing.

Siobhan grudgingly nods. "It is," she says. "It's all about truth." I'm playing a blinder.

"A lot of people would have picked *Harvest*," Eamon says.

"Or *Goldrush*," adds Norman.

It looks like plain sailing until Methadone Miriam snaps out of her trance. She turns the beads of her eyes in my direction. "My friend Jenny Hayden says you're a punk."

I immediately laugh. "Who, me? Do I look like a punk?"

The hippies study me like lab assistants peering through a microscope, but there are no bondage pants, there's no spiky hair. The uniforms are gone, the paraphernalia stashed away, the rituals few and far between. These days, punks are invisible, living out their lives in angry retreat, like Nazis in Bolivia.

Norman comes to the table with a giant mug of tea. He sits down and slurps. He looks at me without flinching, and says, "That's quite a serious accusation."

Siobhan nods and adjusts her breasts. "We can't have punks in the house," she says. She has no problem with rats, mice or cockroaches. Just punks.

"She saw you coming out of the Roxy in Covent Garden," insists Miriam, "wearing a torn jacket covered in safety pins."

What a night that was. The band flung themselves around the stage like marionettes in the hands of an epileptic. They crashed into instruments and they bashed into each other. Noise fused with music and burst from the wire-covered speakers like a fist, smacking the punching bags made from fishnet and black leatherette. Women with Picasso eyes wrapped themselves around boys with Lowry bodies. The floor was a sticky pin-cushion for stiletto heels and the walls were scrawled with mascara and magic marker. It was heaven, decorated as hell.

The band blistered through a twenty-minute set, then left the stage, cursing the audience. The lead singer gave us the finger and screamed, "WANKERS – WANKERS – WANKERS!"

I was the one who set up the chant in response: "AMADÁN – AMADÁN – AMADÁN."

Without understanding, the crowd joined in: "OM-MA-DAWN – OMMA-DAWN – OMMA-DAWN."

The lead singer, lost under the barrage, skulked away. The roof of the Roxy lifted and blew out the steam over Neal Street. On the other side of a cold sea, Brother Tyrell slept in his single bed, his frock hanging like a headless ghost beside him. Worn-out after a hard day's work – beating children is a young man's game – he would never know that somewhere in the world his least promising pupil, against all odds, was keeping the language alive.

"Well," persists Miriam. "Is it true? Are you a punk?"

I smile at her because I always stay calm when confronted with the truth. Then I laugh at the preposterous suggestion and slap the table, making the hippies jump, and this is when the little miracle occurs. A bluebottle fly, long dead but still clinging to the ceiling, hit by the shock-wave of the slap on the table, suddenly disconnects, plummets downward and plops right into the middle of Norman's tea. Norman stares for a moment, and then laughs. Eamon laughs. Siobhan explodes; her body convulses. Even Miriam chuckles, and for a minute forgets she's craving a needle to embroider pleasure inside her veins. The mood in the kitchen is so light we could almost float away.

Eamon nods at Norman, who goes to the stereo and selects an album with Neil Young on the cover. The turntable turns and the speakers crackle. Sinead lights a patchouli incense stick and waves it around. Miriam reaches across the table and touches my hand. "Everything is cool," she says. "Everything is cool and wonderful."

Eamon produces a house key and lays it on the table in front of me. I pick it up and put it in my pocket. A pitiful whinge fills up the kitchen. The hippies sing about Knights in Armour,

Mother Nature and Silver Spaceships. To ensure my place in this household, I move my lips and pretend to know the words. I do my best to smile through the pain.

26

SKIN

I stood at the counter in The Jubilee Clock and waited for Noel Reddy to show up. Two dull-witted men chalked their cues and walked around the game like Hajis circling the Kabaa. They smacked the cue ball into clusters of stripes and solids, but nothing went down. The barmaid lazily turned pages of the *Sun*, fanning her face with boredom.

Noel Reddy owed me a half-ounce of blow, and he was proving difficult to track down. It didn't surprise me. Most Paddies turn into the Scarlet Pimpernel when confronted by a creditor. In Ireland, a cheque is something you give somebody *instead of* money, a paper diversion drawn on the Bank of Go-Get-Fucked.

The black ball rolled prematurely into the middle pocket. One man cursed and the other man whooped. Five pounds changed hands and the losing player came to sit on a stool beside me. "Your turn, if you're interested."

I told him I wasn't. We got into a conversation about the stupidity of life and he told me he was a merchant seaman. He had been everywhere, or at least everywhere there was water, and now he was home for a week. He wasn't expected, and a neighbour had told him that his wife had taken off for Albufeira. "If I find out she's been gone with a bloke, I'll put both her legs in hospital, I will."

He asked me if I'd ever been disappointed in love, and I said no because I didn't want to feed his misery. He was young enough to be interested in drugs, so we had that much in common. He had sucked mescaline buttons in Ecuador and chewed khat on the horn of Africa.

"All that stuff makes me constipated," he said with a sniff. Londoners always sniff to emphasize their disappointment.

I asked him where I might get some dope.

"Nothing 'round here, but if you don't mind going up the Farm, I know a bloke who will fix you proper."

He was referring to the flats at Broadwater Farm.

"Place is full of nig-nogs," he sniffed, "but you might be all right, you being a Paddy."

Impeccable logic.

He wrote a name and address around the outer edge of a beer-mat. "Tell him Charley Moore sent you."

The 149 bus was full of poor people generating cancer. The smoke moved around slowly, like dirty water in a fish-tank. I took a window seat upstairs and stared out at the same glum house cloned a million times.

"Ticket?" said the bus conductor, looking at me with eyes as empty as a ballerina's fridge. I gave him twenty pence in exchange for a long ribbon of paper covered with smudged hieroglyphs. "Ticket?" he said to the old woman in front of me. She clipped open her purse and poked at the pennies inside.

When I'm on a bus, I always end up back in Ireland. I don't know why my head wants to go there because the rest of me certainly doesn't. I often return to the first time I saw Kim Sutton, stepping out of a Morris Oxford in the Rainy Town. She didn't bother looking looking left or right on Dublin Street because she knew the traffic would stop. The traffic always stopped for Kim Sutton. She was a sexy Moses dividing a Red Sea of Ford Escorts and rusty Datsuns, and her followers weren't Israelites but middle-aged men enchanted by her teenage curves. They would have followed her into the nearby river Barrow, and out the other side. They would have chased her all the way to the Atlantic, their hands in their pockets and their heads lost in lust. She could have drowned a whole town of dirty old men.

She went into Morrison's shop. I followed. I picked up a packet of Wrigley's and stood behind her. I didn't even like chewing gum: two minutes of flavour followed by a disposal problem. Kim Sutton wore faded jeans and a tight black polo neck sweater. Her hair was tossed, tangled and twisted like beaten flax. No make-up. Braided thread on her wrist, signifying something I didn't understand. Outside, the traffic stayed stopped and the drivers clenched their steering wheels waiting for her to re-emerge. Nan Morrison stood behind the till and smiled shyly. She was a sixty-year-old virgin spinster who had never considered lesbianism until this moment.

"Anything else?"

"I'll take the *Evening Press*," Kim Sutton said, reaching for the purple masthead.

"Is that the lot?"

There was a pause. She knew I was standing behind her. She squared her shoulders in a what-the-hell fashion. "S-Ts. For my mother," she said.

Nan was the one who blushed as she pushed the bulky packet of Southalls into a brown bag that just wasn't big enough. The paper split. Nan's fingers fumbled. The packet of feminine protection tumbled onto the floor. Nan tried to cover it with her body, like a soldier taking a grenade for the rest of the platoon.

"I have a bigger bag out in the back," said Nan, exiting with the offending item practically tucked under her jumper. Kim Sutton turned and looked at me. Her voice was flat and expressionless. "Yes," she said, "this *is* actually happening."

"You have dimples," I said. "Two of them."

"They usually come in pairs."

Nan returned with a big brown bag and Kim Sutton left the shop. I wondered if we'd ever meet again. Nan stood scowling behind the counter, tapping the register with her money-stained fingers. She looked me up and down as if she'd sell me by the pound.

"You should be ashamed of yourself," she said, her lips as tight as a fighter's fist. "Watching!"

I slipped a stick of chewing gum into my mouth and folded it with my tongue. She blushed and looked away.

"Ashamed," she said.

I blew a small bubble and burst it.

"Ashamed," she said.

Outside, the traffic started moving again and the horny men squeezed their gear sticks. They would follow Kim Sutton wherever she went.

"Ticket?" said the conductor.

"Are you buyin' or sellin'?" An Irish voice rose like the sound of an annoying musical instrument.

"Ticket?" repeated the conductor.

"I thought maybe you had concert tickets." The Irishman stood. He wobbled and wavered as he slapped his pockets in search of change. "Hold your horses. The money is on the way. Can I post it to you? Would you accept an IOU?"

He had the whitest skin available to the human race, whiter than the bone beneath. A Celtic pattern scrolled down a forearm and unfurled at a cuff. He was a work of art, drawn by ninth-century monks on vellum, interlaced and illuminated, conveying a message to future generations.

"Bollix!" said the pale, pissed Paddy when his money tumbled onto the floor. He got on his knees and laughed. He held up a fifty-pence coin and the bus conductor wound out the ribbon of paper. The Irishman stood, shook his electrified curls, then stuffed a ten-pound note in one of his pockets and a five-pound note in the other. "Giving money to an Irishman," he roared, "is like giving a machine gun to a chimpanzee." He made a rat-tat-tat gesture as he sprayed the bus with an imaginary Uzi.

The bus approached a muddy demolition site and the half-ruin of a corner shop teetering sideways. It looked like the battle of the Somme, but with cement mixers rather than artillery. The wrecking ball swung and swiped at a gable. The Irishman jumped up from his seat and waved a lump-hammer speckled with mortar. He was Thor and Bacchus rolled into one.

"Destruchtion boys. Destruchtion."

People smiled, but nervously.

"Conor McDonagh has come to town," he yelped. "You'll put them up and I'll pull them down. Hah!"

The bucket of a JCB ripped out a window sash.

"Yiz are all cunts," he roared, then he caught my eye. "But not you, boy, not you." He smacked a dusty seat with his hammer. "Not you."

An invisible wire connects everything Irish in London. We all oscillate on the same frequency. We know each other by our gait and the tilt of our heads, the tucked shoulders and the thumbs hooked in pockets. Show me a man striking a match, and I'll tell you what county he hails from. We are a class unto ourselves in this land. Put us in a donkey jacket or a dinner jacket, it doesn't matter. We can't hide the savage within.

The other passengers began to shrink. Now they were surrounded. This thing was like a virus. One had turned into two. Could there be more? The woman with the clear plastic headscarf and the bright red lipstick. Would she suddenly jump on a seat and cry, "Hup the IRA!"? What about the man with the bushy eyebrows and the paisley cravat? Was he stowing a sawn-off shotgun wrapped in a copy of *Republican News* and loaded with buckshot made from Rosary Beads?

Ding-ding.

"My stop!" roared the Irishman, and then he tumbled down the stairs and rolled off the bus. He braced his shoulders and tossed the amber thatch on his head. He smacked a metal pole with his lump hammer and made it sing. He tilted his ghostly face upwards and shouted at the passengers, "Hah, hah, hah! Yiz re all cunts." He caught my eye. "But not you boyo, not you."

The graffiti on the wall outside Broadwater Farm said, IF YOU BELIEVE IN GOD, YOU'LL BELIEVE IN ANYTHING. Two young boys kicked a red plastic football, so light it stayed in the air for ages. One of them looked at me and said, "Oi, what you doing around here, mate?"

I told him I was looking for young children to murder and eat. He went very quiet. Before the ball returned to earth, he and his friend were gone.

Somewhere, music boomed. I had been in the Broadwater flats once before with my mate Kevin. He'd bought a cassette deck from a junkie with scorched eyes. "You give a druggie more than twenty pounds for anything," said Kevin, "you're throwing away money. A score for a score, that's the score."

I came to the source of the music. Beyond a window, a man and a woman danced close together to a belting riff. He wore a white shirt, stiff as a board with Robin starch. Her dress ran down her body like water and pooled on the floor, dangerously close to the hi-fi socket. Poor people always have the best stereo equipment.

I watched them as they swerved around their living room, grinding their bodies, skanking on the off-beat, swinging their hips on the riddim backflow, thrusting and lusting on the rising bubble. They were the blackest people I had ever seen, a mixture of Caribbean and coal dust, and they were in love, or they were stoned. Sometimes it's hard to tell the difference. In both cases, people spend too much time licking their lips.

Boom, boom, boom! went the reggae music.

A Morris Marina with rust bursting from ruptured blisters sat on concrete blocks outside the flat. Inside the car, two cats with their backs to each other dozed on the passenger seat. The dancing couple paused and looked in my direction.

Wayah-wayah-wayah! went the reggae music.

The black man came barefoot to the door and stepped out onto cold concrete. He looked up at an open window where a teenage boy held a lit match and a firework.

"Baby, are you trying to burn down da whole estate?"

The boy grinned as he drew a bright spark from the touch paper. "Nah mate," he replied. "Just your pad."

The black man put his hands on his hips and laughed, but

two seconds later the rocket whistled across the passageway and almost burned a hole in his tangled dreads.

Fubba-fubba-fubba! went the reggae music.

The black man's girlfriend turned the rod on the venetian blinds and the white slats cut across her sleek body. She became a zebra.

The boy was shocked by his own action. His knuckle sprang to his lips and his eyes opened wide. He looked like he wanted to dig a great big hole and fill it with his fear. The black man said nothing. He didn't curse. He popped the boot on the Marina, pulled out a tyre iron and flexed a muscle full of boiling blood. The tyre iron flipped majestically through the air, missed the boys's face by six inches and took a cup-sized lump out of the concrete cladding.

Ketcha-ketcha-ketcha! went the reggae music.

The boy disappeared into the flat and the window slammed shut. The black man turned in my direction. "What you looking at?" he said.

"Charley Moore sent me."

The black man smiled. His name was Arnold and soon he would sell me a glassine wrap of PCP dust. But the thing I liked most about him? He had dimples.

27

LOST

The hippies evicted me this morning. They had a pow-wow at the crack of dawn – 11am – and decided I should go, taking my bad vibrations with me. Since my arrival, the geyser has exploded and a truck flattened the neighbour's cat. Wherever I go, I bring death and cold water.

Last night, I arrived home at close to midnight. I usually just head straight for my room, but a voice, half-stoned and thick with stupidity, called out from behind the kitchen door. "Hey Barry? That you? Come on in. Someone here we want you to meet."

Against my better judgment, I entered the greasy kitchen. A bunch of hairy-heads sat around the table, smoking weed that smelled depressingly home-grown.

"Come on in, dude," said Eamon. "We just got some great grass from Chiswick."

Suspicions confirmed.

"Sit down, man, sit down."

In a hippie house you soon master the art of sitting on a smelly chair without actually touching it. I call it hygienic levitation.

"This is my cousin, Judy," said Eamon, indicating a small, pale girl who barely existed.

"Hi," she said in a tiny voice

"Hi," I replied, sensing that all was not well in the universe. I got the feeling I was about to be *Judied*. I declined the offer of a smoke because I had a nice bedtime block of hash in my pocket, and no intention of sharing. The talk was the usual hippie-dippy shite, a mixture of astrology, herbal claptrap and suspenseful tales from the dole office. Eventually Eamon asked if I wouldn't mind joining him on the steps. We went outside and watched the moon hook one of the Battersea chimneys.

"Nice girl, Judy," said Eamon, as if he had just met her for the first time. He started rolling a cigarette. "We were thinking," he said. "Maybe, um, you'd be cool with sleeping on the sofa and giving Judy your room for the next few weeks?"

"You've got plenty of space in your room."

"That wouldn't be cool, man. She's my cousin." The moon tugged on the Battersea chimney as Eamon put a match to his wobbly cigarette. He sucked. The glow lit up his pasty face and turned him into a leering Guy Fawkes on a bonfire. "I wasn't going to tell you this, man, but she just lost a baby," he said.

Hippies are vessels for misery. "Poor Andy. His caravan was hit by lightning: now he's living upside down in a tea chest"; or "Pascal caught an ear infection from his pet macaw, and the bird keeps laughing at him." It's always something dumb and depressing. You never have a hippie come up to you and say, "You know Kevin with the poncho? He just won five hundred quid in a raffle."

"Really?" I said.

Eamon looked at me with sad-dog eyes. "It's just for a few weeks," he said finally.

I realised a counter-proposal was expected. "Tell you what," I said. "I've got two beds in my room. If she wants to sleep in the other one..."

"Okay dude, that's cool," he said, then turned and went back into the house.

I lay in bed with a portable Olivetti and a joint and started writing bullshit, childhood stuff. Half-remembered tales of Mrs Best. She was the woman who did the weekly cleaning in our house in the Rainy Town. She rode a big black bicycle with a child seat on the back and a front wheel that needed oil.

Squeak, squeak. Squeaky squeak.

When you heard that noise, you knew she was coming. With adults, she was all respect and propriety, but she shared the darker side of her soul with children. She promised us revenge on all the unfairness in the world.

At six years of age, I was thrown out of school by the Mercy nuns. "Pack your bag and get out of here," screamed a red-faced nun. I didn't even have a bag. I had a pencil and a pink copybook with Jesus dying on the front. I left the school and walked to the junction of Green Lane and Station Road, which I wasn't allowed to cross. I sat down on a low wall and waited.

Squeak, squeak. Squeaky squeak.

Mrs Best appeared, and when I told her what happened her face lit up with fury. She crouched down beside me and whispered, "You tell me if this ever happens again. I'll put my fist up that nun's arse and I'll pull out her guts." She put me into the child seat on the back of the bicycle and brought me to the bakery shop for a lemonade float. She smoked a cigarette and watched me suck.

A few years later, when I was on my way home from National School: *Squeak, squeak. Squeaky squeak.*

Mrs Best pulled up to the kerb and asked about my teacher, Mr Bentley. He had a savage reputation, and would often beat the entire class just for the physical exercise. His face was purple, his lips were huge, and his jaw belonged on a donkey.

"If he lays a hand on you," Mrs Best said, "you tell me and I'll snap him like a twig. I'll ate him up and you won't even find the bones."

I knew I could call her in at any time. She was the protector beyond the periphery, the human atomic bomb, and if I ever pressed the button, she would turn our wet town into a hot Nagasaki.

The door opened and Judy entered. I continued typing. She had changed into an oversized T-shirt with *Atomkraft Nein Danke* on the front. She asked if everything was okay and I said it was fine.

"What are you writing?"

"My life story."

"Is it long?"

"Nine pages if I die tonight."

She slipped into the bed across the room and studied me.

"You're not like the other people in this house," she said.

I agreed.

"You look like you should be famous," she said.

I agreed with her again, but I wondered how it was possible to be nineteen and still talk like a twelve-year-old. I put the portable typewriter down beside the bed and rolled another joint.

"Do you have a girlfriend?" she asked.

"I've just been dumped," I replied.

"Me too!" She said it with such enthusiasm, it sounded like a good thing. She was full of questions. She asked about the small leather bag that held all my possessions. I told her I travelled light. I never packed a conscience.

She asked if she could read my work, and I said okay, but as she leafed through the world of Mrs Best I could see her eyes grow wider and wider. She had never seen such quiet savagery in a woman. "Did she ever get married?" she asked.

"No. She lived with her brother. He was discharged from the army for doing something despicable in the Congo."

I offered her the joint. She took two short puffs that never reached her lungs. I took it back and finished it, then turned out the light.

"Do you believe in God?" whispered Judy in the darkness.

I told her I had been an altar boy for two years. My surplice had a lace collar and when I held a flaming taper I looked like an angel, but sometimes I drank the consecrated wine.

Her shock rippled across the room. "How did it taste?"

"It was the blood of Jesus," I said, "but it still tasted like piss."

I woke up to find Judy slipping into bed beside me.

"I don't want anything," she said, but people always say that and they always want something. She had more questions. "Why were the nuns so mean? Did they hate children?"

"No," I said. "It wasn't children they hated, but men."

People always hate what they can't have.

"Every nun, when she lies in her cell at night, mumbles prayers and benedictions in the quest for peaceful sleep, but inside her head she has one word screaming around in tiny tormented circles."

"What is it?" she asked.

"The word," I said, "is COCK, COCK, COCK, COCK, COCK, COCK, COCK, COCK, COCK, COCK, COCK, COCK, COCK, COCK, COCK, COCK, COCK, COCK!"

We both laughed, but I knew the irreverence caused her discomfort. A moment passed, then she confessed.

"I was pregnant."

"I know," I said. "Eamon told me."

She took my hand and placed it on her belly. I wasn't sure how I felt about touching a chamber that had so recently hosted death, but I let her guide my fingers in gentle circles around her navel.

"I don't want anything," she repeated.

I was glad because I had nothing to give.

"Why did she have a child seat on the back of the bike if she had no children?" she asked.

I had no answer for that.

She pushed herself against me. I thought about her pale skin. Most Irish girls look like corpses. I felt something stir and I couldn't contain it. I tried thinking sympathetic thoughts in the hope that it would make the damn thing go down, but something hardened and it wasn't my resolve.

She was a mother who had lost a child and her blood was pounding inside her head. Her boyfriend was probably in bed with somebody else, she was in bed with somebody else, and nothing made sense. I turned a little sideways and tucked myself back in retreat.

"I couldn't have been a mother," she said.

I searched for the appropriate reply, and in a gesture not typical of me, offered a small raft of sympathy. "No," I said. "You would have been a good mother."

She started to sniffle. "I wouldn't," she said, like a petulant child. "I couldn't have been."

I wasn't sure which way to go. "You would've been great," I said.

"Why are you saying that?" she moaned. "Why are you torturing me?"

There was something missing and I couldn't figure it out.

"You're just trying to be cruel," she sobbed.

"I'm just telling you what I think. I can see you as a wonderful mother, doing all sorts of wonderful motherly stuff."

She lifted my hand from her belly and pushed it away. In the process, her fingers glanced against the upright soldier.

"Oh my God!" she said. "Oh my God!"

Before I knew what was happening, she was out of bed and retreating. The door opened and then slammed. I lay there, confused, trying to make sense of the senseless. I repeated aloud my portion of the conversation.

"You would have been a good mother."

"You would have been great."

"I can see you as a wonderful mother, doing all sorts of wonderful motherly stuff."

That was me at my very nicest. What had gone wrong?

Ten minutes later, Eamon stormed into my room.

"What you just did," he spluttered. "It was so uncool."

"I'm sorry," I shrugged, gesturing towards the regimental mascot under the sheet. "Fucking thing has a life of its own." His blank expression told me that we were talking about two different things. "What exactly is the problem?" I asked.

"The problem," he said, "is you telling my cousin what a great mother she would have been when the poor girl has just had an abortion."

"You told me she 'lost' a baby."

"It's a euphemism," he said.

"No it isn't, you fucking moron!" I said, getting up out of bed. "When you have a foetus sucked out of you and into a vacuum cleaner, you can't really call it 'lost'. You know where it is. 'Lost' is a fucking tragedy, it is not a surgical procedure." I couldn't believe how dumb these people were. They just tossed their words into the air and let them fly in the face of reason.

Eamon backed away in embarrassment, or possibly the sight of a semi-erection scared him.

"An appointment at the Marie Stopes clinic," I continued, "is not a 'misfortune' or a 'mishap'. It's a bloke with rubber gloves fiddling around with your privates, and he's not there to 'pick fruit' or 'sort out the plumbing' or 'trim the wick'. He's there to kill a baby. Do you get it? Huh? Do you fucking get it?"

Maybe I overdid it. From across the hall in Eamon's room came the sound of Judy sobbing. One by one, hippie doors creaked open. *Squeak, squeak. Squeaky squeak.*

The world was a big empty place, a void with me at its centre. And no Mrs Best to rescue me.

28

CHIN

In fifteen minutes I will lose my job, so I need to look my best. This Bond Street haircut cost £23, and the man with the scissors called me "darling sir". I'm wearing a newly-purchased pair of grey cord pants, a Sun-Yat-Sen jacket and black boots with Cuban heels. In the office bathroom, I study myself in the mirror. I tilt my head until the perfect blend of insouciance and arrogance is achieved. I aim for a regal appearance, more Bourbon than Windsor – Louis XVI, say, before his wonderful chin ended up in a basket on Place de la Concorde.

The Christmas before I left Ireland, I had some poetry published in a brown paper bag of a magazine. The publisher, a well-known figurative painter, invited me over to the west of Ireland for a night in Limerick city. His sidekick was an eminent professor visiting from America. When they looked at me, they were like a couple of bears wondering how they'd go about opening a tin of salmon.

"I love your poetry," said the professor. "It reminds me so much of my dear, dead friend, Pat Kavanagh."

"Mmmm, I would like to paint you some time," said the artist.

We moved through a variety of the city's seedier bars. Along the way, we picked up a playwright – the professor's cousin. He said yah instead of yes, and for the first ten minutes, I thought he was German.

The professor said, "I'm just back from Haiti."

"What took you to Haiti?" I asked.

"There isn't a man, woman or child on that island that can't be bought for two dollars." "Mmmm," said the artist.

"Yah," said the playwright.

The artist was on a tour of the western region, painting portraits of elderly pint-suckers in bars. Whenever he found an interesting face covered in warts and windburn, he would buy the specimen a drink and sketch his slurping mouth. "Mmmm, wonderful cranial structure," he would say as he rendered the thirsty savage in charcoal sweeps of *chiaroscuro*.

The playwright told us about his most recent production for the National Theatre. It dealt with contemporary Irish issues, seen through the eyes of an ancient, immortal hero. It was a re-evaluation of social mores and deep-rooted misconceptions, turned under the loupe of sardonic observation.

Fucking yawn.

"Contrary to populist belief, we are the engineers of our own misfortune," he said, drawing an overflowing bucket from his well of self-satisfaction. "We fail to see the beneficence of external authority, the cultural gifts bestowed by a greater power – our erstwhile imperial masters." "Bollocks," I said. "The problem with looking at our history through rose-coloured glasses is that you don't see the blood dripping from the Union Jack."

"Yah... You know you should have been a writer... instead of a fucking poet." The playwright burned me with his eyes, then departed without finishing his drink.

The professor tipped back a glass of rum. "You remind me so much of my dear, dead friend, Bill Yeats."

We fled to a hotel bar close to the railway station where we settled into leatherette banquettes. The artist and the professor began to use even more extravagant gestures, as though their wrists had become double-jointed.

"You remind me so much of my dear, dead friend, Freddie MacNeice," said the professor.

"Mmmm," said the artist. "When I look at you I really want to get out my brush."

It transpired that we were waiting for another man to join us. Referred to as Liam-Francis, he was due in on the 9pm train. The artist and the professor argued over who would meet him in the station. Neither of them wanted to leave me with the other.

"You should go. You've known him longest."

"But you know him best."

"He likes you more than he likes me."

"You're taller. He'll see you above the crowd."

I said I'd go and meet him myself. All I needed was a description.

"Mmmm," said the artist. "He looks like a leprechaun."

"He looks like a leprechaun who mends shoes," added the professor.

"He looks like a leprechaun who mends shoes, but he's not very successful," said the artist.

The professor took a swig of his drink. "He looks like a leprechaun who mends shoes. He's not very successful and he lives with a paralysed mother."

"He looks like a shoe-mending leprechaun, not very successful, lives with a paralysed mother and is afraid to go to the village dance because the young girls mock him."

People around us began to join in.

An unsteady man leaned over and sputtered, "He looks like a leprechaun, mends shoes, not very good at it, lives with a crippled Mammy. The young girls at the village dance mock him because he always forgets to zip up his fly."

"He looks like a leprechaun, bad shoe repairs, Mammy in the attic and when he goes to the village dance, his langer is always hanging out."

Gales of laughter, interrupted by the bar owner, who said, "Keep it clean lads, there's women on the premises," which of course wasn't true.

The air carried by the Shannon River was fresh and welcome. I waited on the platform as the night birds flitted above, weaving in and out between the rusty roof trusses and the toxic recesses in the asbestos sheeting. Irish train stations are windy sheds full of oily men waving red lanterns like whores on the prowl. The waiting rooms are caves decorated with ingrained dirt, outdated timetables and muddy sections ripped from the Farmer's Journal. Half the light bulbs are blown, their tungsten filaments dangling like tattered webs. Dead ash and cinders spill from hearths where fires are never seen burning. Whispers of abandonment and the echo of half-hearted farewells fill every nook and cranny. The only thing colder than an Irish train station is an English marriage.

A headlight appeared and then dimmed as the black-and-amber diesel rolled into view. The tannoy announcement sounded like a man in the midst of castration, begging to be left with one ball. A few people disembarked. Some students, a woman with rowdy, uncombed children and a bunch of confused tourists who obviously hadn't read the warnings in the guidebook. Then he appeared, a tiny man with a giant green cap on his head. He looked like a frog sheltering under a dock leaf. His skin was lumpy and his hair unruly. His clothes were older than fashion itself, his boots carved from solid blocks of leather. He carried a tiny suitcase, held together by a pair of mismatched belts.

"Liam-Francis?" I asked.

He spun around and looked at me, clutching his tiny suitcase tight to his chest. "I don't know you," he said.

I explained that I was with the artist and the professor. He backed himself against a girder as a cloud of confusion spread across his face. "But... but... How did you recognise me?"

I told him it was just a lucky guess.

He pulled himself out of the shadows and studied me. "You have a magnificent chin," he said.

"Are you another artist?" I asked.

"I'm an Irish dancing master," he replied, striking a dramatic pose. I have performed before the Mayor of Boston. I give exhibitions and provide entertainment at wakes."

The little fucker was serious.

"Lead on," he said. "I'm dying for a pint."

"Indeed," I said. "And there's a whole pub full of people dying to make your acquaintance."

I exit the gents bathroom and walk down the linoleum runway between drawing boards. People avoid my eyes because they know I'm already halfway out the door. I'm a ghost, but a noisy one because of the clicking Cuban heels. I step into the model room, where chief engineer Alan Mack awaits. There are no chairs, so we both sit side-by-side on the floor, the miniature world of

Windscale/Sellafield laid out before us. A cluster of cotton-wool trees line the banks of the Calder river, and the pile chimneys tower above everything, like two remaining legs of a vanished coffee table. Alan offers me a bag of crisps. Salt-and-vinegar.

"I never have time to eat, old boy," he says. "So I live on crisps and jars of pickled onions."

I notice my drawings spread out in an area close to the miniature car park. They are slashed with thick red marks.

Alan munches on a crisp. "The boffins in Ruislip have a problem with your drawings, Barry."

"All of them?" I ask.

"Even those that are not yet conceived. I'm afraid you've gone and stamped on the sausage, Barry, and you cannot mess with the boffins' sausage."

As usual, I do not understand his metaphor.

"*Ad fucking oculos*, Barry. Plain for the world to see."

He picks up one of my drawings, a gully detail in the medium level decontamination area. "You made a right hairy dildo out of this one, old chum," he says, dropping it into my lap. "It appears that the dimensions you've added to this drawing actually come from a different dimension. Draughtmanship, Barry, is like accountancy. The numbers must add up. Your numbers do not add up. I have an old sheepdog, Barry, and she could piss better information than you have on this sheet."

I nod. I'm not embarrassed. I'm just amazed they didn't catch me out sooner.

"We are both shallow men, Barry. I'm afraid I'm so shallow, sometimes my depths rise above my surface, but it's my job to look after the sausage. I am the keeper of the sausage, Barry, the high-priest of the porcine tube, the ganger of the banger. I'm sure you understand."

Not even remotely.

He lights a cigarillo and flicks the match towards the green tinted water in the Magnox Storage Pond. The match sizzles and goes out. Almost simultaneously, the rain starts tapping on the flat roof above our heads.

"Do you get much rain in Ireland? I'm quite geographically ignorant. Your lot could be going around in ponchos and sleeping under banana trees, for all I know. God I hate the damn rain. First thing to wear out on an English car are the fucking windshield wipers. I should visit some time. Ireland, I mean. I've heard Belfast described as Manchester with petrol bombs, or maybe that was Glasgow. Some places have always been a mystery to me, like Chingford. I've never been, but I imagine it's full of Chinese."

A crash of thunder sounds directly overhead.

"I wish it wouldn't do that. It makes this whole business seem so damn ominous."

"Any chance of a reprieve?" I ask, even though I already know the answer.

"Afraid not, old bean. They'll come down on me like a fat man on a ballerina if I don't hack off your scalp and wag it out the window. The problem lies with the boffins, Barry, the boffins. We're dealing here with the deadliest elements known to man – Polonium, Actinium, Rubidium, the stuff that hides underneath the periodic table and growls – and we can't have some innu-merate Paddy chewing his pencil and fucking with the laws of physics. Their words, not mine. Well, actually, they're my words."

He takes a thick rubber band off his wrist and flicks it at a cooling tower. It wobbles but does not fall down.

"We get paid according the number of bums on seats, but unfortunately, your bum has become unseated. I really don't want to lose your bum. I like your bum. Not romantically – I'm happily married to a very unhappy woman – but fiscally and logistically, I need your bum."

He bursts open another packet of salt-and-vinegar.

"When the Egyptians built the pyramids, Barry, they expected them to last for ten thousand years." He points an outsize crisp at the Windscale complex. "We'll have to bury this place for just as long to make it safe." He looks around to make sure we are alone. "They're blaming you for the fire," he says.

"Which one?"

"July 17. Six men injured. Mucho Becquerels floating about the Cumbrian countryside. Don't eat the grass and don't drink the milk. They're probably shooting the mad moo-cows as we speak."

"I'm not responsible for that."

"Of course not, but you know the old expression: 'When in doubt, hang the Irishman.'"

I light a cigarette and Alan crunches his crisps. He wipes his lips with a greasy corner of his cardigan.

"Barry, old chum, my personal belief is that you should pursue a career somewhere beyond the boundaries of civil engineering, perhaps in the world of photographic modelling. You've got a damn fine chin."

"So I've been told."

"Some wonderful careers have been built on chins. Our American friends are very keen on the mandible. I can see you on a Hollywood balcony, a Maserati in your driveway, a naked woman clad only in a pair of those strap-on angel wings lying on your tossed bed. The phone rings insistently. It's your agent. A three-picture deal..."

Alan is lost in fantasy, but I don't interrupt because, frankly, I like the picture he's painting. If I had known being fired was this much fun, I would have done it more often.

"At the Oscars, Barry, you won't thank the Academy. They'll thank you. Starlets will write their telephone numbers on brassieres with red lipstick, and then catapult them in your direction. You'll cruise Sunset Boulevard with the top down and the golden statuette perched on your dashboard."

He crunches his last crisp.

"You'll be sipping mimosas poolside in the Chateau Marmont while my missus has me hooked up to a catheter, watering the begonias. You'll be at the end of the rainbow, Barry, and I'll be a crock."

The spark in his eye fizzles and goes out.

"That's it then?" I ask.

"'Fraid so."

The rain stops and the sudden quiet leaves an emptiness between us. Alan scrunches his crisp bag and tosses it, like a grenade, at the reactor casing. He makes a schoolboy exploding noise, followed by the wee-wah of an ambulance. He grabs my hand and it's like squeezing a damp, pungent sponge. "Toodle-oodle old poodle."

I leave the model room and walk back through the drawing office. Nobody pays me any attention. The glass door closes with a hiss of farewell. The Grand Union canal oozes under the Uxbridge Road as I walk up the ramp to the bus stop, but it seems crazy to wait for public transport when I'm on my way to stardom, fortune and fast Maseratis. I light up a joint and the air around me turns blue and shimmery. I flick back an expensive haircut and point a magnificent chin in the direction of Ealing Broadway. I move with a quickening click-clack of Cuban heels.

Into a golden future.

26

DUST

The last time I smoked PCP it nearly killed me. It was time to do it again.

Kaye stood in the middle of the living room and said, "Did I just say that? Did I?"

Blind Boy had no idea what she meant. "Did you just say what?" he asked.

"I don't know. I thought you were listening. When some people talk, other people listen."

The Phencyclidine was dragging her down into a bad place, a basement without stairs.

"You're in a basement without stairs," I said, and that really freaked her out.

"Why would you say that? What is this stuff?"

"PCP," I said, "dust from the wings of an angel."

"Angels are scary," she said. "I've always been spooked by angels. I bet you knew that. I bet you did."

"What about your guardian angel?" I asked.

"My guardian angel was a bitch. She did mean things. Once, she tried to push me under a lorry."

We were in Wilkinson House, a pre-war block of flats that overlooked Kennington Oval. After the hippies tossed me out, I asked Blind Boy and his girlfriend, Kaye, if I could stay with them. Sure, they said, for a week. I liked that. Friendship with a time limit.

"I might have to go to the hospital," said Kaye. "I'm hearing my ears. They're making squeaky noises"

"Maybe you have mice," I suggested.

Blind Boy laughed.

"Why are you laughing? Don't laugh at me."

Kaye went to the window and pressed her forehead against the cool glass.

"Is she crying?" he asked.

"No," I said.

"She sounds like she's ready to start."

Kaye picked up a hairbrush from the sill and marched back across the room. "Here," she said, thrusting the brush into my hand. "Brush my hair."

"Are you talking to me?" asked Blind Boy.

"Hardly. You wouldn't even be able to find my fucking head."

"She's a piece of work, isn't she?" said Blind Boy.

"Why would I brush your hair?" I asked.

"Because it relaxes me and because you're the one who messed me up with that fucking PDP."

"It's PCP," corrected Blind Boy. "PDP refers to the Piecewise Deterministic Process, which is part of probability theory."

"In all probability, I'm going to smack you if you say another word," she said as she knelt down before me.

"I fancied Kim Sutton," she said. "When we were at school. I was a class below her, but I fancied her like mad."

Blind Boy's mouth dropped open. "I didn't know you had 'tendencies,'" he said, but she ignored him.

"Once, she tied a ribbon around my wrist, a silky blue ribbon. I thought it was the coolest thing ever.

"Did you ever *do* anything, the two of you?" asked Blind Boy, his tongue lolling out the side of his mouth.

"What is that supposed to mean? I was fourteen years old! Look at your tongue. I wish you could see yourself."

"Me too," he said. "Me too."

I brushed Kaye's hair and watched it crackle with electricity. Blind Boy sat back and listened to the slow swiping noise. He never removed his dark glasses; he didn't like spooking people. Kaye held up the palm of her hand in front of me, in a gesture that looked like a foreign salute. She took the index finger on my free hand and used it to inscribe slow circles on her palm. Blind Boy tilted his head. Could he sense the sex in the air? The bastard gave nothing away.

"When I listen to Margaret Thatcher," he said, "I hear a woman who is disappointed with men. When she was young, she trusted men, she wanted them to rule the world, but when she found they were lacking, she decided to rule it herself."

Blind Boy tilted his head to the other side. He was all over the place. "Do you see this watch?" he said. "People often wonder why I wear a watch. Why would a blind boy even bother?"

He tapped his wristwatch. Kaye and I continued our ritual of touch.

"I bought this watch with my confirmation loot. I paid for it with coins and stacked them on the jeweller's counter. He had a satin mat that deadened the sound of the money. Three pounds, four shillings and sixpence. 'Good boy,' he said, every time I added a coin to the mat. 'Good boy.'

"His wife came out from behind the counter, and the jeweller said, 'This chap is buying a watch with his confirmation money, isn't he the big man now?'

"I wasn't that big. I could feel everything towering around me, especially the grandfather clocks. I ran my fingers over the watches and picked one out. The jeweller said, 'Will you be okay with the Roman numerals?' As if it made any difference."

Kaye pressed her hand against my fingertip and mouthed three words: "I WANT YOU." I mouthed the same three words right back.

"The watch had a metal strap and it needed a link or two removed. They led me into a little workshop behind a curtain. I could feel the wagging finger of a Bunsen burner close by. I could hear a snipping pliers and the sound of emery cloth rubbing on metal. He told me I would have to wind it every day, but I shouldn't over-wind it."

Kaye took my finger and pressed it against her torso. Her sternum felt hard, as if she were impaled on a steel post. She slid my hand sideways to her breast and circled the softness.

"'How will I know when I'm close to over-winding?' I asked. 'If you feel resistance,' said the jeweller, 'you may have already gone too far. In that case, just bring it back. I have ways of unwinding watches. I can turn back time.'"

I could feel the energy in Kaye's nipple asserting itself through the cloth. The air tightened around us. Blind Boy continued to talk about his watch.

"I walked down the main street with one sleeve rolled up. I hoped that somebody would ask me the time, and then I would show them. I went to the bridge. I stood on the bridge and

210

listened to the water. You search for a pattern but there's never a pattern in the sound of water. A man stood beside me and said, 'There's a bunch of plastic dollies caught in that weir and they look like drowning babies. They're blinking and smiling and waving.' I think he was drunk. I held out my arm but he didn't ask the time. I walked uptown, past the cake shop, the shoe shop, and the pawnshop, but nobody asked. People brushed past, but nobody asked and then the siren blew in the sugar factory yard and the whole fucking town knew the time. And there was no point anymore."

Kaye opened her mouth and showed me her tongue. I slipped a finger into her mouth and the skin healed up around it.

"I've thought about losing the watch, dropping it in the street or a pub, but things never end well in this town when an Irishman leaves something ticking behind him."

Blind Boy pulled off his dark glasses and I wondered if the two dead pits could sense what was happening, what had been happening since the night of my arrival. The games we had played in circles around him. The penetrating glances and the crude gestures a body makes when it needs another body. Did he know that Kaye left the bathroom door open when she showered? She washed as I watched through the steamy soft focus. Had he noticed the way we sniffed each other whenever we passed in a doorway? Could he hear the words we never spoke and the long, charged spaces between them? Treachery and deception crawled on its belly and brushed against his heels. Did he feel it slither? He was too nice a guy to know the truth. Deceit is the greatest drug of them all.

Without any warning, Blind Boy rolled up his sleeve and forced his arm between us. The watch face loomed as big as the moon, but I no longer understood the Roman numerals. What the fuck was "X"? Did it mark a spot? Was is a generation or a brand? A dirty movie? A kiss at the end of a letter? A failed exam? An illiterate signature? An unknown quantity? X-Ray, X-chromosome or X-fucking girlfriend? I stared at the watch and tried to make sense.

"Ask me what time it is, Barry. Go on. Ask me the time."

His tone was hard and sharp. I slid my finger from his girlfriend's mouth and it popped like a cork pulled from a bottle.

"What time is it, Blind Boy?"

"It's time for you to leave, Barry. Time for you to fucking leave."

I stood, wobbled, and left the flat. I didn't look back.

I was homeless on Harleyford Street, a draughtsman without a plan. I headed towards the Oval. A black man in dreadlocks came bouncing towards me. He looked like he had springs in his shoes and hinges on his knees, and it made me wonder, why do Irishmen always walk as if they're pushing a wheelbarrow?

"I have to go to France," I declared.

"Bon voyage, mate," he said.

I carried on walking around the Oval. The red-brick wall on my right held giant graffiti words, a backward sentence that stretched on forever. It asked a profound question that no one could answer: WHATEVER HAPPENED TO SLADE?

I keep walking around the Oval, past Clayton Street and Bowling Green Street. I saw a man in dreadlocks coming towards me. Was it a new black man or the old black man?

"I have to go to France," I said.

"I know," he replied.

Outside the tube station, I started to peak. Every noise turned into a scream, every footfall was like a jack-hammer on the pavement. I grabbed a railing and held on tight. I was afraid if I let go I'd sink into the ground. I couldn't catch my breath. Some-body asked, "are you alright?" and I replied, "never felt better." I turned to see who was speaking, and it was Jesus. Not just a bloke with a beard, but Hollywood Jesus with the golden glow and the Persil robe. I told him I wanted to believe in him again, but he said it was all right if I didn't.

"I need to get to France," I said.

"*Mais oui,*" he replied. "*La Ville-Lumière vous attend.*"

I was surprised. You never imagine Jesus speaking French.

"Will you help me?" I asked.

He smiled his godly smile and snapped his fingers. I felt something pop between my shoulder blades, a knot of muscle opening like a rose, bones fusing and forming into a magnifi-cent tangle as my jacket filled with a great unfurling. I flexed and flapped and felt my toes lift from the concrete. I knew I could fly. I knew I could fly all the way to Paris because now I had the wings of an angel.

27

BLACK

The dental surgery was in Earl's Court, next door to the Cole-herne gay bar, and the air was heavy with the smell of poppers, Jack Daniels and holster oil.

Bob the dentist was Australian. He held the x-ray up to the light box. "You on any medication, mate?"

"No," I said, even though my brain was puffed up like a kiddie pool.

"What you have here," he said, "is a serious abscess. It needs to be drained, cleaned and treated."

"Just take it out," I said.

After a few weak protestations, he gave me a shot of something warm and fuzzy. "That good?"

"Oh yeah," I said. "All I need now is a deck chair and some decent reggae music."

He snorted with laughter as he lit me up with the yellow horseshoe bulb. "Are you completely numb?" he asked.

Been that way for years, I thought.

He stuck a heavy pair of forceps into my mouth and yanked until something cracked. "Fuck!" he said. His brow rippled and his lips tightened. The tooth came out in four jagged shards and each piece tinkled as it landed in the stainless steel pan. "What do you think of the English, Barry?"

He had pliers in my mouth, so I couldn't answer, but I would have told him they were okay, in moderation.

"You know, when a Pom goes out for a drive, he doesn't look at the scenery – he looks at the fucking petrol gauge. That's his life. Starts out full, ends up empty."

I felt some blood trickle down my throat and I wondered if it was possible to drink yourself dry. Bob put his face very close to mine. I didn't want to hear any more antipodean opinions, and maybe he sensed that. He pushed my tongue aside with a metal spatula.

"Couple of stitches, mate." He worked away for ten or fifteen minutes and then said, "That'll be forty quid."

I stood up and paid him.

"Remember, that's an open wound in your mouth, so if you're popping into the poof bar, I wouldn't be doing any of that." He made a vulgar fellating gesture.

Four hours later, I'm on my way to France. The train for Newhaven pulls out of Victoria station at 9:05 pm. It's a rolling dustball on wheels, powered by a Morris-Oxford three-cylinder lawn-mower engine. The compartments smell as if somebody has opened a tin of human sweat, poured it over a wet dog and fanned it with a chip butty. Also the driver could go on strike at any minute and jump from his cab, shaking a clenched, oil-stained fist and screaming anti-Thatcher slogans.

On the plus side, I have an entire compartment to myself.

I don't have any luggage, just a change of underwear in one jacket pocket and a toothpaste tube in the other.

We flick past a cemetery and I think of the Rainy Town. Dwyer's Monumental Sculptors. Their window display of mock headstones, commemorating people who never really died. People who never really lived. The inscriptions are so sad that sometimes townsfolk stand outside the shop and weep:

ANTHONY REED, DIED IN INFANCY.
AGED THREE YEARS. MOURNED BY
HIS MOTHER, FATHER, SISTER KATE
AND NANA.
'SAIL, SMALL BOY, ON THE PAPER BOAT
OF OUR PRAYERS.'

I don't feel well. I close my eyes. The conductor announces, "We are now stopping at Eastwoods...Salfor...Horley..." It's one long platform that runs through my dreams.

The compartment door slides open. I keep my eyes shut. I hear the voices of black women.

"Nobody here except for one pretty skinny boy and he's all asleep like a babe in the woods."

They come in and unpack themselves all around me. The quiet is killed by the sound of crinkled plastic bags and low gurgling laughter.

"Are you awake? Hey skinny boy. Yoo-hoo! Skinny boy, are you awake?"

I open my eyes and say, "I am now."

"Ooh! I think he's cross because we woke him up."

"Very cross and very skinny. What a combination."

"What's your name, skinny boy?"

"Barry."

"I think we prefer Skinny Boy."

There are three of them, sisters, two in their mid-twenties and one about my age. They introduce themselves. Laura, Sylvia and the girl my age is Sonia.

"But everybody calls her Sunny."

"Our dad gave us names that end in aaaah! Because he says that's the sound of pleasure."

"The sound he made when he was making us."

Laura and Sylvia laugh at their own naughtiness, but Sunny turns away in embarrassment.

"Where are you going?"

"I'm going to France," I say. "Paris."

"Are you French?"

"I'm Irish."

Laura leans across the compartment and squeezes my knee. "We do love the Irish," she says.

"They say the Irish invented the English language. Is that true?" asks Sylvia.

Before I get a chance to answer, Sonia speaks. "I have to apologise for my family. You were all nice and private in here and then we came along."

Laura and Sylvia begin again. "We talk all the time. It's incessant."

"Continuous."

"Constant and uninterrupted."

"No chance for anyone else to get a word in edgeways."

"Our dad says we're like sirens."

"The ones on top of the ambulance."

They shriek and bump shoulders together. They whisper in each other's ears. Sonia shakes her head in dismay as Sylvia probes further: "If you're going to France, let me ask you this, how come you don't have any baggage?"

I show her my toothpaste tube.

"Mmm. A boy needs fresh breath if he's going to kiss a girl."

"Now you're taking it way too far," Sonia says.

"Listen to little sister. You think she never kissed a boy in her life."

"You should come back to our house."

"Our daddy is a professor at King's College."

"Mama could feed you up with hushpuppies and saltfish."

"Jerk chicken and Run Down stew."

"Calabaza and callaloo."

"Bammies 'n' patties."

"Don't forget the Mannish Water."

"It's an aphrodisiac."

"He needs to put on some weight if he wants to be a proper son-in-law."

"He can stay the night."

"Of course. He has his own toothpaste."

"What a treat for little sister Sunny. She could be your hot water bottle. She has never before been with an Irishman."

"And I've never been with a..." I stop in mid-sentence. Everything drags to a halt. Only moments ago, these women were laughing, joking and teasing each other, but now they turn curious and strangely disappointed. The sentence can only end one way because I don't know their ethnicity. I don't know if it's Jamaican, Trinidadian or Barbadian. Maybe they're not even West Indian.

"I've never been with a..."

Laura, Sylvia and Sonia look at me and wait, but I can't finish it now. I can't say the obvious words. They hang in the space between us like a dead bird on a wire. Normally I don't care if I behave like a jerk, but this feels different. There is only one avenue of retreat: I close my eyes and pretend to sleep. I listen to their silence and inside my head I repeat the mantra, "Hushpuppies and saltfish. Jerk chicken and Run Down stew. Calabaza and Callaloo." And then I sleep.

"Hayward Heath... Plumpton... Cooksbridge... Lewes... Newhaven."

I wake up and the girls are gone. Noise erupts everywhere: Forklifts and cranes. Whistles. Shouts. Announcements. I join a line for the traditional frisk and tickle. A greasy-looking woman with a lumpy bra directs me to an immigration official behind the vinyl curtain.

"Please take a seat and empty the contents of your pockets on the table."

I scoop out everything I own: a one-way ticket to France; £22 and some change; my pocket knife, underwear, passport and toothpaste.

The man on the other side of the desk has spent too much time in the sea air. His skin is bright red. He's turning into a lobster. He extends a pincer and prods my possessions. "Twenty-two quid? Is that all you've got?"

"Yeah," I say, "I thought there would be more myself."

He switches out the blade on the knife. "It's a flick knife."

"Yeah, I know."

"It's illegal."

"Not in France."

"But you're not in France."

He opens the toothpaste tube and squeezes out a striped inch. "Spearmint. Don't care for it myself." He picks up the passport and skims through it from the back. "You've got some missing pages here."

I vaguely remember being beaten up by the Brilliantined Levantines, lying on the floor in Gloucester Place as one of them sprinkles me with green paper.

"Passport isn't valid unless it's completely intact. This document is useless."

"I need to get to France."

"Too bad, mate. The only place you're going is back to where you came from." He slams the passport down on the table. "Do you have any other form of picture ID?"

I open my jacket to reveal, clipped on the inside pocket, a BNFL identification tag.

He reads the words slowly. "British. Nuclear. Fuels. Limited." He unfastens the tag and holds it up alongside my face. "That's you all right." His expression says, *How did an ignorant Paddy land a cushy job in a fancy office in a place without seagulls and birdshit?* And my expression replies, *I have no fucking idea.*

He pushes my possessions back across the table.

An hour later I'm standing at the stern of a ship beside a frozen flag. I am the only man on deck. I unroll the tin tube of toothpaste and wiggle the blade inside. Out pops the plastic wrap. The powder sparkles under the cold moonlight. Four sharp snorts of crystalline snow and it's Christmas in my nose. I look at the knife before I fold it away. Am I crazy enough to do something stupid or stupid enough to do something crazy? Is there a difference?

A port and a starboard lighthouse slash their beams at one another like illuminated swordsmen. They cleave the sea with their mighty swipes and their blades come up glistening, dripping with the lifeblood of the English Channel. Smoke pulses out from the towering stacks and everything trembles: the rail, the lifeboat, the capstans, and me.

I think of Laura, Sylvia and Sonia in a house filled with good books and fine cooking. Hushpuppies and saltfish. Jerk chicken and Run Down stew. Calabaza and Callaloo.

"AND I HAVE NEVER BEEN WITH A BLACK WOMAN!" I shout into the vast, deserted sea.

There is no satisfying echo because the water soaks up everything. Even under the cover of darkness, I am ashamed.

28

SOULS

It's 7:15am and the apartment building in Saint-Germain-des-Prés where Kim Sutton lives is still locked. The concierge comes to the window. She pulls a strand of hair back from her face.

"*Bonjour*," she says.

"*Bonjour*," I reply. "*Je suis ici pour visiter ma petite amie.*" I've lifted the sentence straight from a phrase book.

She points at her watch and says "*Huit heures.*"

I find a café and wait. An American-style drugstore across the square is just opening up. One window sign says Marlboro, the other Lucky Strike. The boxy turret on the nearby church is under-ornamented, Calvinist and dour. Aren't the French Catholic? I can't be sure because I didn't listen at school.

The waiter wants to shake hands with me. His fingers are cold and wet. He looks like he has too much energy and this hand-shaking is how he gets rid of it. I don't like being part of somebody's exercise regime. Go outside and do push-ups or

222

run around the block. Masturbate in the men's room, but don't touch me.

I ask for a coffee. He gives me options: café this or café that? I nod. He brings me a cup that belongs in a doll's house. The coffee is bitter and gone in three seconds. He tries to engage me in conversation. I say, "*Je ne parle pas français.*" He tries again, hoping for a sudden transformation in my linguistic abilities. I stare at him and say, "I do not speak fucking French." Thankfully he takes offence and goes away.

I inspect the crinkly French notes I acquired in the bureau de change in the railway station. I like them – all Racine, Voltaire and Berlioz – but I get the feeling they won't go very far. This is a problem because, apart from the mixture of PCP, dentist dope and Sealink speed still raging through my system, I don't have any more medication. It is the furthest I've ever been from a source. How would I even go about getting more? "*Excusez-moi, monsieur. Avez-vous junk?*" Is it like buying dope in England, where everyone with tattoos and six children is a dealer? I don't know.

The waiter returns with a plastic saucer containing my bill. "English?" he asks.

I nod and confirm his hatred for the wrong race.

Outside the church, a woman takes baskets from the back of a Citroën van. Her husband or boyfriend sits in the driver's seat with a cigarette slouching between his lips. I do not like his look: the languid wave of greasy hair and the beaky nose with oversized nostrils. He watches her in the rear-view mirror like a pimp observing a lazy whore.

I'd like to hit him. To pull him out onto the cobbles and kick him in the cobblers. I'd like to bind him hand and foot, toss him into the back of the van and roll it into the Seine. I'd watch his panicky face in the back window, his giant nostrils steaming up the glass. I often think thoughts like this. Is it normal? Does everybody want to murder everybody? Should I be concerned?

The woman arranges the baskets outside the church. She puts up a wooden sign that says "*Fleuriste*"and her companion drives away.

I look at the baskets and think of Baudelaire. *Les Fleurs du Mal*.

And I remember how my bad habits started with a friend in a field full of flowers.

"Opium is just like turnips or spuds," said Tom Kavanagh. "You weed it, you water it, and you walk away from it. There isn't going to be any funny business because funny business would land the pair of you in reform school."

Eight acres of bursting poppies leaned one way and then the other under a blue Irish sky. My friend Paul and I were sixteen years old and we didn't have enough grey matter between us to form one small sensible idea. We were dumber than the day was long, and this was high summer, 1975. Standing on the headland, we did our best to conceal our stupidity in a haze of cigarette smoke.

"We'll drop the hut down before lunch so you have some place to get out of the sun," said Tom Kavanagh. "But don't be spending all day inside, or it'll be taken away just as quickly. Am I making myself clear?"

We nodded our vacant heads.

Tom Kavanagh turned and left the field. He could have opened the five-barred gate but he chose instead to vault the wire. It might have been a cool move for a younger man, but he snagged the tip of his boot and fell on his face, and then didn't look back because he knew we were snickering. He got into the old Commer pickup and drove away, humiliated.

"What a moron," said Paul. "I can't believe I'm putting up with this shite for twelve quid a week."

"Twelve quid," I echoed, and then we both laughed and laughed until it wasn't funny anymore. Paul spat on his hands as if he were about to do some serious work, but then he just leaned on his hoe and looked off towards the hills.

"Pink Floyd play Knebworth in July," he said.

We looked at the flowers rolling like ocean waves and said nothing for quite a while. A little after twelve o'clock, a flatbed lorry pulled up with our hut on the back: an eight-by-eight box made from ship-lapped pine, it smelled of creosote and pipe smoke. The lorry driver and his helper winched it down onto the tarmac, then we had to drag it into the field. I left the door open hoping that it would air out, but the smell was ingrained and refused to depart.

Paul dodged inside. He looked out the window and snarled, "Get off my land!" He pointed the handle of a rake at me and made a *kaboom* noise. I dropped to the ground, clutching my chest. I lay there looking at the cloudless sky, wondering why I wasn't spinning off the planet, into the blueness above.

"Do you believe in gravity?" I asked.

Paul came into my frame of vision. "Do you know anything about this stuff?" he said, nodding towards the poppies.

"Only what I read in the *National Geographic*."

"Do we need any special tools?"

"Just a sharp blade, I think."

He pulled out a Stanley knife and waved it around. "Would you sell your soul to see the Floyd in concert?"

"Sure," I said.

Paul made a slashing gesture across his palm with the Stanley knife and before I could get out of the way, two or three droplets of bright red blood came splashing down on my cheek.

"Hey! What are you doing?" I said, jumping up.

"Let's sign our satanic pact in blood."

"I don't want your blood all over me."

He took a paper tissue out of his pocket and held it tight in his fist. I took the knife and nicked the back of my middle finger.

"Our souls for Pink Floyd and Knebworth," we chanted as we mixed our blood together.

The Angelus bells in the Rainy Town started ringing.

"Wooooohhh!" said Paul in a ghostly warble. "That's the devil clanking his balls together."

"When does he come to pick up our souls?"

"I don't know," said Paul, lighting a match and flicking it into the air. "But probably before we're twenty."

At lunchtime, a stream of cars headed into town. The men and women from the offices in the Agricultural Research Institute looked lost and meaningless as they gripped their steering wheels. Tom Kavanagh cruised past slowly, craning his neck, watching us as we weeded with fake energy. He beeped the horn twice but we didn't look up.

"What a moron," said Paul.

After the last car departed, we got down to business. We slid into the middle of the field, taking care not to leave any obvious path through the poppies. Paul slashed away with the blade and I followed close behind, squeezing the milky juice from the bulbs. After forty-five minutes, we went back to the hut, ate our sandwiches and drank our tea. In two weeks, we had a quantity of gum about the size of a tennis ball. We wrapped it in a supermarket bag and hid it under a cool cluster of dock leaves at the end of the field.

It was Paul who came up with the idea of selling the tennis ball to Wuzzy Ryan. Wuzzy was a red-haired boy with powerless eyes.

He came from a grim home where nothing ever worked out. There was an older brother called Scuzzy and a younger sister called Huzzy. Scuzzy was kicked out of the army after less than two months, when they discovered he had a tendency to hurt people while they were asleep. Huzzy was a scary combination of shapeliness and mental retardation. Whenever she answered the dog-scratched door to their council home, she would turn sideways, making you squeeze past her speed bumps. She licked her lips and batted her eyelids, a lot. It was as if a space alien had hijacked a human body, but never learned to work it properly. Paul once summed up the family by saying that somebody had broken into their gene shed and robbed a bunch of chromosomes.

Wuzzy was alone in the house when we called. He had just painted his bedroom walls with one thin coat of "midnight sky" emulsion. Blotches of the previous colour showed through, like pasty skin under a black nylon stocking. We sat on the bed. Wuzzy weighed the tennis ball in his hand. He batted his eyes and licked his lips. In the semi-darkness he looked just like his crazy sister, only without the speed bumps. He gave us £40 and six tabs of acid that he kept in the middle of a Sven Hassel book. We were on our way to Knebworth.

Three years later, just before I left Ireland for good, I ran into Paul coming out of a bookie shop in the Rainy Town. He was counting money.

"Did you win?" I asked.

"Nah! Just counting what I didn't lose."

I asked him if he was working and he said, "People who hire people don't hire people like me."

We'd taken different paths after that summer in the fields. He had dived into a bad world where people stole each other's televisions and forged each other's signatures. These people owned dogs that never stopped barking and children that never stopped crying. These people were not recreational users; they were occupational users. Narcotics was their day job.

"Recently I've been getting the feeling that somebody is standing behind me," Paul said. "You ever get anything like that?"

I told him I didn't.

"It's like something permanent and dark is hovering behind me. I think I know what it is, but I'm afraid to say."

"Really?" I said, looking for a way around him on the footpath.

"Do you ever think about your soul?"

I thought he was joking, so I turned up the sole of my shoe for a moment and studied it

"I'm worried about damnation," he said. "You know... Knebworth."

I didn't remember much about that episode. Before we got on the ferry to England, we dropped the acid and smoked a small blob of opium we had kept. Somewhere outside Chester, everything started to blur. I vaguely recalled running down a street shouting, "Thank you Satan," while Paul charged along beside me, going, "You're a top man Satan, top man."

"It must get to you," he persisted.

I told him I had to go, but he was blocking my way. His eyes flicked around and he was biting his lips. "I think the devil is behind us," he said. "I know you feel it too. Look at the way the town has slowed down all around us, traffic standing still, birds stopped in mid-air. You know, I can hear things. I can hear your heart beating, the blood running around in your veins, the thoughts jumping across the tiny spaces inside your head. Remember the field, the hut, the Stanley knife, the blood. The bargain with Lucifer?"

"I'm in a hurry," I said.

"We're both empty canisters, spiritual voids forced to walk around this arse of a town, eating, drinking, smoking and backing horses."

"I don't back horses," I said.

His face fell in disappointment, but he pressed on. "I know how we can win back our souls," he said.

I wanted to laugh in his face, but for all I knew, he still had that Stanley knife.

"The 4:25 at Newmarket, there's a horse called Mephistophilly. Long shot, fifty-to-one, but it's a sign. Me running into you like this? Another sign."

"How much do you need?" I asked.

He looked hurt. He tilted his head like a puzzled dog. "Don't you get it? This is a chance for us to redeem our spiritual essence. How could you even put a price on something like that? An opportunity to pull the burning disks out of the eternal flame and dip them in the ice-cold water of deliverance? You think that's about money?"

"How much do you fucking want?" I said.

He shrank back. "A tenner would do," he said.

I gave him five and told him to leave me out of it; the devil could keep my soul. He took the note and folded it. He pressed it into his palm and then closed his fist like a magician. He was about to make money disappear. He turned and went back into the bookies. A bunch of wasted men stood looking up at the speaker, listening to the numbers and the odds. Paul joined them. He took a seat in the corner of the shop, closed his eyes, and waited for the race to start.

29

BLOOD

FRIDAY, DECEMBER 21, 1979

The florist outside the church at Saint-Germain-des-Prés holds up a cluster of blue stuff. "*Anemone hépatique*," she says.

I nod.

"*Pied d'alouette*," she says, brandishing some yellow stuff.

I nod again.

"Lily?" she says, in uncertain English. "For truth and honour?"

"Best skip that," I say.

I go for a dozen roses and something she calls "*les pois de senteur*". She wraps the bunch, adds a bow, two little bells and some sparkly sprinkles. All of a sudden I look like I'm on my way to a gay funeral.

"How much?" I ask, holding out my crinkly notes.

She takes the lot and gives me three coins in change.

"*Au revoir*," she says.

The concierge answers the door on Rue Jacob. I take a rose from the unwieldy bunch and hand it to her.

"*Elle est jolie*," she says.

I tell her she is *jolie* too which of course she isn't. She turns bright red and I am surprised. I didn't think middle-aged people could blush.

"*Cinquième étage, chambre vingt-six*," she says, pointing towards the service entrance.

I go to the stairs. In my head, jostling with the poison, is a voice from my childhood. Sister Euphrasia. A champion of conservative Catholicism. Whenever she blessed herself she made the sign of the swastika, and every one of her utterances both started and finished with an interrogative: "What are you doing, boy? In the name of all that is holy, what?"

"I have no idea," I say aloud.

I stop at the second landing and look out at the courtyard. The concierge stands in a beam of sunlight looking at the rose.

I don't feel well. My toothache is back. I need something to calm me down. Maybe one of those tranquiliser darts they shoot at elephants. Throw a net over me and strap me to the front of a Jeep.

A door opens on the third floor and a teenager with a punky haircut appears. He has the look of someone on the run, like an Irish boy dodging a pregnant girlfriend. Insertion followed by desertion. He glowers when he sees me. Do I look like a burglar? Would a burglar be carrying a giant bunch of flowers? In France, probably yes.

My jaw explodes with every heartbeat.

Two more floors to go. I need a sherpa. "McKinley reached the summit and planted the Irish flag. Tensing Norgay followed close behind, bearing an enormous bouquet."

This journey seemed like a good idea a long time ago. Yesterday? I can't recall. I've perdued a lot of temps since then. I'm angry. Irishmen are always angry. They're always asking each other outside for fights. It's why there are no submarines in the Irish navy.

As a draughtsman, I can see a cross section through this entire building: the joists, doorjambs, twisted coils of electrical cable, voids filled with mouse droppings, concealed lead piping wrapped in blankets of asbestos, men in showers, teenagers lounging in beds, small dogs in baskets, tables littered with empty wine bottles, bedrooms choked with clothing.

Two potted plants and a child's scooter on the fourth-floor landing. Shoes outside a door. The smell of coffee. Laughter. Joy. Happiness? Is this France or did I get on the wrong boat?

I look out through the landing window and the concierge is dancing with her flower. Yes, it's France.

I stand outside number twenty-six with a pumping heart. I turn the doorknob and to my surprise, the door opens.

The room is tiny. The window takes up most of one wall, a washbasin and bookcase another. She has taped some of her monotone paintings above the headboard: ballet dancers and teapots rendered in splashes of gouache and Indian ink. Beside the bed, on a table with short legs, is *Iron in the Soul* by Sartre, who also had short legs.

There is something heart-shaped on the floor beside the bed, no bigger than a thumb nail. Perhaps it has fallen out of a pocket. I know what it is, but I pretend to myself that I don't.

In a white sweatshirt with a tangle of strawberry blonde curls spilling like foam across the pillow, she is perfectly still. Her fingers clutch the outside edge of the sheet, but the rest of her is hidden beneath a mound of heavy blankets.

"Kim," I say in a voice that never leaves my mouth.

I stand in the doorway and watch her sleep. I used to do this when we lived together. I was fascinated by the peace she brought into a room, the silent calm. I'd smoke a joint and watch her breathe. It was television with the sound turned down and the sexiness turned up. Way up.

"Kim," I say, and the word comes out as a whisper. She stirs and tightens her grip on the sheet. "It's Barry."

Her brow furrows. I say nothing more and she relaxes. I think of the early morning sex we used to have in London. I called it mornication.

"Kim," I say again, and this time the volume startles me.

Her eyes open wide and she screams. She sits upright in the bed. "Oh my God! What are you doing here?"

It isn't a promising start.

"How did you get this address?"

"Good morning to you, too."

We look at one another and the room closes in. The ceiling comes down and brushes the top of my head. The walls reach out and touch each other. She clears her throat. She takes a sip of water from a glass on the windowsill. "Why are you here? You have to go," she says.

"Why didn't you tell me you were leaving London?" I ask.

A look of incredulity sweeps across her face, opening her mouth and narrowing her eyes. "Why? Because you were the one I was getting away from. Now, please go!"

"Kim, I've come a long way."

"I can't believe you just walked in."

"Well, the door was open."

She blanks her expression. She does this when she wants to change the subject.

"You look a fright," she says.

"You look beautiful," I reply.

Maybe she softens a little, but there is no sign of surrender. I look at the heart-shaped plectrum on the floor. She follows my gaze. And we both know the truth. I bend down and retrieve it.

"Learning to play the guitar?" I say.

She looks out the window and I talk to the back of her head.

"You had somebody here last night," I say. "Was he French?"

"American." she replies.

I picture a gladiatorial guitar slinger with the Stars and Stripes tattooed on his ample chest and power chords pumping from him amplifier.

"A boyfriend?"

"No. In fact I just met him last night, in Polly Magoo's."

"I see. Now you're fucking strangers you meet in bars? I suppose it's a good way to make some extra pocket money."

She doesn't rise to the provocation. The house pitches and yaws as if it has been hit by a giant wave. I half expect to look out the window and see a rising tide, carrying the dancing, drowning concierge.

"Please. Go," she says. "I don't want to ask you again."

"You haven't told me why."

She fixes me with something that looks like pity. "I left you because you were a monster. Not a big monster, just a small, nasty monster. I left you because I was tired of...."

I stop listening. I look at the book on the bedside table. The cover shows a horned man with a bloodied sword and a bag of human heads slung over his shoulder. I really want to beat the shit out of Sartre. I imagine I'm thumping him and he calls for back-up. Samuel Beckett joins the fray. "I will not let you strike the little man," he says as he puts up his fists like a Trinity Protestant. Boom! Kick to the knee, low punch to the testicles and Ireland's greatest living playwright goes down like a sack of *pommes de terre*.

"You never listen to me," Kim says. "You're not even listening to me now."

"Well at least the sex was good," I say.

"No," she said. Sex with you wasn't like sex. It was as if you were stabbing me."

"Oh yeah? Well I never heard anybody say, 'Yes, yes! Right there! That's the spot!' when they were being stabbed."

I slip my hand into my pocket and pull out the switchblade to illustrate the point. Kim is shocked and silent and I am aware of the terrible contrast between love and sharp steel. I have to do something with the blade, now that it's out. A knife has certain needs. I start shredding the flowers. The leaves and the petals fall to the ground in a tumble of mixed colours. It strikes me that, with all my rages and tantrums, I've never seen her look this scared. I shred and I shred until nothing remains. A cluster of flowers at my feet, I'm a junkie Thérèse of Lisieux, lit by a yellow beam of sunlight rising over a courtyard gable.

Then there is blood. It falls on the flowers and splashes my shoes. I look in the mirror and see the stream oozing from my mouth and running down my chin. The stitches have burst and the pain is released. Now I know why vampires smile.

Kim backs into the corner and wraps herself in a cocoon of blanket. I am not a small monster. I am a monstrous monster. Size is always important.

On Rue Bonaparte, a man walks towards me carrying a poodle in a shopping bag. The dog stares straight at me and I am filled with a resentment directed at all things canine and all things French. If I had my own shopping bag it would contain an angry Irish setter with sharp fangs and a hunger for toy dogs. Sean the setter would devour Pierre the poodle and wash him down with black frothy water from a Parisian puddle.

The man smiles as he passes me. I feel exposed. When you

take away an Irishman's anger, you're left with nothing but a bare, quivering skeleton. I reach Quai de Conti where the *bouquinistes* are laying out their antique porn and *bandes dessinées* for the lonely men in dark sunglasses. I spot the Pont des Arts, half a bridge going nowhere.

I ask a man on the quayside, "*Où est le reste du pont?*"

"It collapsed when it was hit by a barge," he replies in English

"Fucking French drivers," I say.

He walks away. Will nobody fight with me?

I reach the Pont Neuf and the statue of Henry IV. Down the steps to the Square du Vert Galant, the arrowhead at the tip of the Île de la Cité. I sit on the bench and watch the heavy barges struggle against the river. It's a nice place to relax and swallow some blood. I look at the heart-shaped plectrum I kept as a souvenir. I flip it over and discover the motto stamped on the back: "I PICK YOU."

I start to laugh. It's the sort of laugh that drives away people and pigeons.

"PLUCK YOU TOO," I say as I toss the heart in the river.

It's quiet except for the voices.

"You have to stop," Kim said before I left.

"Stop what?"

"Stop this."

"I can't. I have to keep going until everything is…"

"Everything is what?"

"Everything is broken."

A police launch goes past on the river with a siren blaring and blue lights flashing. When the sound subsides, I hear another voice, harsh and probing, devoid of pity. It belongs to Sister Euphrasia. Her words bounce off the Pont Neuf and Notre Dame cathedral, they echo over the copper rooftops with their fired clay flues. The question is given to the entire city of Paris, but of course there is no answer.

"Where will you go now, boy? In the name of Jesus, Mary and Joseph, where?"

ACKNOWLEDGEMENTS

A special thanks to Julian, Susie, Charlie, Mark, Margaret & Nollaig, and all at The Story House Ireland.